NAPLES, FL WASHING

LOOSEN YOUR LOTUS

Opening Your Heart to Self-Discovery and Peace

B.A. CRISP

2Portal Publishing

The publisher is not responsible for websites (or their content) that are not owned by the publisher.

Cover/interior by Ashley Ruggirello/www.cardboardmonet.com

2 Portal Publishing provides this author for speaking engagements. Tolearn more, please email: dcrisp@2portalpublishing.com

Library of Congress Cataloging—in—Publication Data

Crisp, BA 1966-Loosen Your Lotus: Opening Your Heart to Self-Discovery & Peace/Crisp BA Crisp.—First Edition p. cm.—(A Cosmic Truths Book)

ISBN 978-1-7343087-6-1 (paperback) 978-1-7343087-5-4 (e-book).

1. Personal Growth

2. Self-Transformation 3. Conduct of Life 4. Spirituality 5. Philosophy 6. Metaphysics

I. Title II. Crisp, B.A. 1966- Cosmic truths book.

Non-Fiction. LCCN: 2023912317

Printed in the U.S.A.

TABLE OF CONTENTS

Dedicated to Max Kashani

in Memory of Rumi
for reminding me that LOVE is our purpose here...

In Memory of Sgt. Linda Pierre
KIA
April 16, 2011
Forward Operating Base Gamberi,
Nangarhar Province, Afghanistan

A book of thought to see you through.
When times are tough, and friends seem few.
See the message in these pages true,
In a gift of ***Love*** from me to you.
When I am gone, my days all through,
Think of me and read anew.
Within this book, please read deep.
And in your heart, I'll always keep.
—BA Crisp

FOREWORD

"It's funny how life happens," Sgt. Linda Pierre said in a video she posted on YouTube in 2009. *"What I said I would never consider, that I would never do, is what I've come to love, which is being a soldier."*

To quote Sgt. Linda Pierre, it is funny how life happens, and it is interesting for many reasons I am writing this foreword.

B.A. Crisp is not only dedicating this book of love and self-discovery to the memory of a young soldier who died in combat, but she is asking for a foreword from an old warrior. This fact may unfold differently for every reader as you navigate the pages and stories of this extraordinary book. It hits me personally in the face as I craft this dedication to what feels like the antithesis of what I have come to know of life—combat, killing, rescuing, and the art of the masculine.

I would offer I am B.A.'s yang to this work—the understanding of death and saving lives as my own personal testimony. As you read her powerfully written stories, I invite you to consider your own understanding of war and death, rescue and resurrection, life, and love, and find an understanding as I did from B.A.'s words–internal conflict, external conflict, the culture of winning and no option of losing, and how these things all affect us and specifically you. I invite you to explore this juxtaposition of life and death and self-actualization against the mundane as far as feels comfortable, or rather, uncomfortable, for you.

In this book, B.A. Crisp takes you on a journey like nothing else I have ever experienced. Her beautiful Buddhist undertones are matched with a disarming humor and the undeniably indomitable spirit of a survivor. Through her journey, she explores with us love, success, failure, positives and negatives of coercion, fear and ultimately–enlightenment (ideally).

B.A.'s manuscript came to me at a pivotal moment in my life—I am retiring from the Air Force, walking away from the warrior ethos of the special operations aircrew I have been blessed to be a part of for over twenty years, and walking into a new phase of my life.

"*New phase of my life*" are the five words I have used to reduce the anxiety of this giant life change for myself and for my family, even though I get the feeling my five-word veneer is fragile and vulnerable to even the slightest of challenges.

B.A. reached out to me in a way that must have been calculated by the universe to ask me to write this foreword. She and I hadn't spoken in months—I assume it was due to her dedication to writing this book—but she wanted me to write this part. I am humbled. God speaks to us all in different ways, however you define *God* and however you define *speaks*. It's a personal choice to decide how to listen.

B.A. anchored her request for my foreword in the passing of her friend Sgt. Linda Pierre. I never met this woman, but I know she represents all of us in the United States military. A small-town girl who didn't know what she wanted to do with her life but found meaning and purpose in the Army. Linda represents so many who serve. Her passing in a suicide bombing reminds me of her ultimate sacrifice—the one every service member knows could be our own sacrifice in the service to our country.

Sgt. Pierre's story and many others like hers inspired me to co-found The Milieux Project, a 501(c)3 nonprofit dedicated to changing the milieu of Western gender roles by increasing opportunities for young girls to be challenged and learn courage at earlier phases of their lives.

Over the past two decades, there has been a noteworthy rise in the representation of women in the military, with the percentage of female Department of Defense members increasing from 13% to 17%* (source: MilitaryOneSource 2021 study on DoD demographics). These statistics underscore a growing interest in augmenting the presence of women within the armed forces, viewed from various perspectives.

No matter where you stand on women in the military, I personally believe we have not fully understood or embraced the advantages of increasing female demographics. This is not an argument of fairness or equality—the military is no place for a social experiment—but women are a potential national strategic stabilizing force not seen by our nation since President Woodrow Wilson.

Milieux Project is meant to grow more female leaders who will take on these challenges of providing stability and consistency without being distracted into comparative physicality arguments. This book by BA, especially her emphasis of Rumi and the feminine, may be another path illuminated toward a world that embraces our desire to see more strong women in the military, or at least that is my hope.

This manuscript and B.A.'s untethered frankness, joy at life braced against the depths of despair and hardship, remind me of my favorite quote from Henry Thoreau:

"I went to the woods because I wished to live deliberately, to front only the essential facts of life, and see if I could not learn what it had to teach, and not, when I came to die, discover that I had not lived. I did not wish to live what was not life, living is so dear; nor did I wish to practise resignation, unless it was quite necessary. I wanted to live deep and suck out all the marrow of

life, to live so sturdily and Spartan-like as to put to rout all that was not life, to cut a broad swath and shave close, to drive life into a corner, and reduce it to its lowest terms..."

You will not be disappointed to find B.A. is giving you an opportunity to do just that—suck all the marrow out of life; face fear, personal doubt, and whatever challenges you think are holding you back; and loosen your lotus. You will no doubt cry, laugh, and connect deeply with the stories and experiences B.A. shares with you in this book. I challenge you to take the journey fully with B.A. Crisp, to open yourself to the thought-provoking and inspirational ideas she brings to us.

—Jennifer M. Aupke, Col (ret), USAF

To learn more about Milieux Project: https://themilieux.org/

Introduction

"All matter originates and exists only by virtue of a force which brings the particle of an atom to vibration and holds this most minute solar system of the atom together. We must assume behind this force the existence of a conscious and intelligent mind. This mind is the matrix of all matter."

——Max Planck

The Enigma of Our Existence

Life. This four-letter word embodies an intricate and undeniably complex spectrum of experiences, emotions, perceptions, and interpretations. It is a journey where every step unravels new mysteries, questions, and insight. It's part of a grand cosmic mystery humans call *existence*.

Most sentient beings are born into this world with an innate curiosity, an unquenchable thirst to understand the universe and the world we inhabit, and to decipher the ponderous puzzle of our *being*—to answer the question, "Who Am I?" If you know who ***you*** are, pluck this ***YOU*** out of your body and place it in the palm of your hand. If you do not know where the ***YOU*** in your biological container resides, let's unfold your mystery, that place where you struggle in the mud to reach sunlight, so you may become as fully bloomed as the enlightened lotus.

Each one of us is a unique blend of consciousness, matter, body, thoughts, and emotions. We are a symphony and a cacophony of electro-chemical biology and psyche, a masterpiece of nature, an embodiment of the cosmic rhythm of creation, made up at our very core, of energy, frequency, and vibration. Everything of which we are made, chemicals, elements, cells, blood, bone, muscle, electrical impulses, and personality, comes from the cosmos. We have the power to impact the world, and the world, in turn, impacts us. It's how we respond to our world that makes a profound difference in our lives. While each of us is individually unique, we are universally connected as "us", part of a supernatural system, which creates, integrates, and destroys for the sake of Source (however defined). Life is an emanation of this intelligent cosmic soul.

We think, we feel, we dream, we aspire. We love, despair, hope, and fear. We create or destroy, heal, or hurt, inspire, or discourage. The spectrum of human capability is as vast as the cosmos itself, and a testament to the incredible complexity of human nature—a complexity that may be momentarily managed within our illusions, but never completely controlled or capable of perfection.

Our existence is also marked by an ever-persistent polarity. We find ourselves atop the joyous peaks of happiness one moment, only to plummet into the depths of misery the next. We oscillate between wanting the comfort of companionship, to guard against the sting of loneliness, and romanticizing the rugged independence of going it alone, "off-grid." We possess the courage of our convictions but also suffer from our paralysis of doubt. Duality *is* the human existence—a necessary paradox between problems and peace, found within us and "out there." Life is part of a grand multi-universal battle between chaos and order wrapped up in an elusive singularity of harmony, and tucked away in our subconscious.

The Purpose of this Book

Years ago, I had the privilege of serving as a psychiatric assessment specialist at a prominent behavioral health center and metropolitan hospital. In this role, under the direct supervision of medical doctors, my responsibility was to evaluate people being admitted into the psychiatric ward. I was tasked to assess if patients posed a risk to themselves or others, if they were experiencing depression or psychosis, or if they were victims of abuse. I was trained to use a combination of crisis training, de-escalation tactics, and interview questions, where the answers were recorded into a diagnostic software program, an early form of artificial intelligence. Most of the individuals I observed and interviewed were in distress, each enduring major suffering, trapped within unique worlds of perceptions and fear. The predominant approach to treatment was medication management. Without exception, every single patient would typically be prescribed a course of pharmaceutical drugs, often peddled to medical doctors by company reps who offered irresistible perks such as first-class trips to tropical locations or even outright cash bonuses. While these FDA-approved medications might temporarily alleviate the pain and suffering of patients, they rarely provided a lasting solution, and often came with worrying side effects requiring additional meds.

Part of my duties involved conducting daily rounds at the hospital's psychiatric ward, ensuring that patients were attended to according to the bureaucratic and software checkboxes. Nurses dutifully followed doctors' orders and adhered to hospital policies with incredible compassion. Once a patient was discharged, they were usually instructed to attend monthly appointments for medication management at our office. During these brief fifteen-minute sessions, the psychiatrist would adjust or change medication based on the patients' complaints. From my perspective, it seemed like a relentless cycle of non-healing, only serving to perpetuate mental illness and therefore, continued suffering, masked by meds. Patients, my own mother included, often told me they felt *flat* on their meds, experiencing neither highs nor lows, which coincided with dampened creativity or motivation.

Then one day, a talk therapist, a psychologist, joined our team. Through his example, he taught me that people were desperate to be heard, to grow, to achieve good health and functionality, and to release the burdens of their past experiences—and he said—most could heal themselves barring any organic or traumatic brain injuries. Too often, he said, people lacked guidance in coping mechanisms, communication skills, de-escalation techniques, prioritization, or with seeking help to address the kernel of their issues—mostly (but certainly not all) stemming from unresolved traumas. Many patients also faced the challenges of poverty and could not afford their medications. If they discontinued their pills, they would often find themselves back in the psych med management system, caught in what seemed to me, a cruel cycle of physical, financial, and mental dependency sans spiritual, physical, or emotional growth.

I firmly feel that talk therapy, exercise, compassion, support, encouragement, meditation, faith, prayer, security, safety, and in particular, *Love* have the power to level a multitude of playing fields for countless suffering individuals. These elements provide an alternative pathway to healing. I also learned from the esteemed Dr. Bruce Lipton that we all carry baggage, both biologically and subconsciously. Most of this baggage is accumulated during childhood, a period when we are ill-equipped to process negative external influences. We absorb this baggage into our cell membranes, and it shapes the foundation upon which we build our adult lives. I know this because it happened to me.

As a former foster child and ward of the court, I grew up in abject poverty and dysfunction. I endured horrific physical, sexual, and psychological abuse. Yet I can confidently affirm that it is not only possible to change one's circumstances, to elevate mental health and biology, but also to reinvent oneself and rise to new heights, to develop a higher dimensional self in tune with and connected to elevated frequencies. I had to step beyond what I knew, which required stepping inward first.

I invite you on a rewarding and sometimes daunting journey of self-discovery. This safari may lead you to question the purpose and meaning of your life and to seek answers that initially appear beyond reach. Yet within these weeds of endless questions, and our pursuit of excellence and understanding, is an ever-present awareness of our individual and connected existences, which guides us to our celestial nature. This self-awareness is reflected in our resilience, our relentless quest for knowledge, our capacity for empathy and love, our courage to dream, and in our oft-wavering hope for the future.

It is on this safari, with all its complexity, its challenges and reward, that we venture into this book. It is designed to be read from any chapter you choose. Flip the pages and begin. Together, we navigate the landscapes of time, love, dreams, death, and fear. We delve into the realm of God, faith, physics, and consciousness. We explore the intricacies of value, integrity, attachment, and freedom. We seek to comprehend the enigma that is human existence through examples of great triumphs and terrible tragedies. But most importantly, we may enhance our ability to *inner-see* and gain a *first-eye* experience into the realm of limitless potential and *Love*.

Let us embark on this adventure, not in search of definitive answers, or in some fruitless attempt to reach perfection, but in pursuit of deeper questions and meaning. For in the questions, we discover portals to growth, understanding, and ultimately, self-realization and awareness.

In the pages to come, we may not solve even one of life's enigmas or worldly problems, and we will not cure ourselves to perfection. But we will certainly revel in life's mystery, learn from its lessons, and celebrate the divine privilege of being "matter-made." And as such, this makes you and me a valuable part of a grand universal adventure.

Please, bend the rules. Unfasten your seatbelt, fling all judgments and conventions outside the confines of reality, and loosen your lotus...

The Sands of Time

"What then is time? If no one asks me, I know what it is. If I wish to explain it to him who asks, I do not know."
——Saint Augustine

Valuing the Moment: Finding the Profound in the Ordinary

One month after the brutal assault of Hurricane Irma, the Poinciana tree, bruised but unbowed, stubbornly reclaimed its vibrant green form. It unfurled fresh, feathery leaves and fiery red blossoms toward a vast sky. There's quiet joy in witnessing the tree's resilience. It mirrors mine. The bond I share with the Poinciana is profound and personal. I planted it in the front yard years ago, when it was a fragile sapling, a twig, really, practically incapable of standing firm against even the lightest of Gulf breezes. Its crown was shorn off by another storm, leaving it to suffer in its frail and gaunt state, a source of amusement for my neighbors and family who jokingly suggested I give up and replace it with something more pleasing.

Yet with each passing season, the tree, much like me, grew sturdier. It learned to endure the scorching heat, summer subtropical rains, occasional floods, and the fury of hurricanes. My landscaper meticulously trimmed the branches until it resembled a beautiful bonsai tree that might make Buddha envious. When the time was right, the tree and I bloomed in concert, unveiling an inner radiance, a sort of fecund yet welcoming light that lifts spirits and draws humans into both hope and joy. People stopped walking their dogs or driving to take photos of the tree, which they shared with family and friends. Some stood in awe, contemplating its beauty, while others found refuge under its shade, or watched the cardinals and red-chested woodpecker that made it their home.

The tree and I still bore the faded scars of deep wounds, but together, with time, we discovered healing and grew—not into specimens of perfection—but as unique testaments of durability.

Understanding the Impermanence of Time

In our expansive journey through existence, one constant we encounter is change. Change flows through time, an illusional human construct of measurement that chisels and deconstructs bodies (or trees), carves valleys, and sculpts our consciousness. Our life is an intricate yet short dance with this fickle linear force we invented to measure the scope of our *being*. We share a necessary symbiotic relationship on Earth with time, and that relationship often defines who we are and what we become.

The impermanence of time might appear daunting and tragic under the stress of deadlines or when confronted with unexpected accidents, illness, or death. But during a normal day, time should not foster fear or dread within us. Instead, time should inspire us. Time reminds us that every *NOW* is a new canvas, an opportunity to redefine our story, reinvent ourselves, or coat our lives with vibrant hues within reframed self-perspectives.

In each ephemeral moment, we are given the chance to

become our own architects of destiny, to build a shining cathedral of self-awareness upon our past and lay strong foundations of love and wisdom for our future. Sand always slips through the hourglass as long as humans exist to see it, each grain a testament to our fleeting physical nature. But while each grain represents a moment lost, it also signifies strides gained and memories made. Time offers us the opportunity to learn, to grow, to heal, and to evolve before we transition off this planet.

Maybe it helps to view the illusion of time as a wake-up call to action. It reminds us to "seize the day," grasp the moment, and savor the sweetness of breathing. We choose, within time's construct, to be active (or inactive) participants in the blooming narrative of our lives, to craft a story that resonates with our dreams and with the harmony of the universe—or not. Time offers us choices to do, be, or act in certain ways. And every single decision we make ultimately determines where we find ourselves at this moment, in the *Now,* an opportunity for enlightenment, manifestation, and love.

Let us consider the divine lotus. In various spiritual and philosophical traditions, the lotus flower is often used as a symbol of enlightenment that requires patience and time—two assets now in limited supply. A lotus typically grows in adverse conditions. It emerges from mud and then must stretch through murky waters to reach sunlight so it can blossom into a captivating and lasting flower. Lotus flowers are known for their long life. They typically remain in bloom for several days, but their seeds can lie dormant for years before germinating, highlighting their resilience and ability to withstand adverse conditions before realizing brilliant transformation. Additionally, the lotus plant has a flexible stem that allows it to bend with water's movement, resistant to damage from waves and currents. This growth process is considered a metaphor for the spiritual journey of an individual who transcends difficulties to attain enlightenment. The blossoming petals on a lotus represent the unfolding of consciousness and the attainment of inner wisdom. Just as the lotus rises above the impurities of its environment, enlightenment is believed to free individuals from limitations and defilements found in lower vibrational dimensions.

The lotus is rooted in the mud, but its flowers and leaves remain untouched by the dirt and water in which it grows. This characteristic is often associated with the concept of *non-attachment.* In Buddhism, attachment refers to craving or grasping, whether it be toward objects, experiences, jobs, ideas, people, time, or relationships. Attachment is believed to be the root cause of suffering (dukkha) and the cycle of rebirth (samsara). Attachments, Buddhists say, lead to clinging, aversion, fear, anger, resentment, depression, ill health, and ignorance. Attachment perpetuates dissatisfaction and prevents people from realizing their true nature and greater potential.

Consequently, non-attachment does not imply indifference or emotional disengagement. It does not mean we should avoid relationships or altogether shun possessions or ignore illness or injury. Rather, it encourages a balanced and mindful relationship with the world, recognizing that everything is transient and interconnected, including pain, trauma, and attachments. Where there is sickness, there is health, where there is indifference, love too, is found.

Enlightenment involves transcending attachments to worldly desires just as the lotus remains unaffected by its surroundings, even if rooted in them. In Buddhist traditions, some deities associated with enlightenment, such as the Buddha or White Tara, are depicted seated, holding, or standing on a fully bloomed lotus flower. This representation symbolizes an awakened state or an ability to rise above suffering and its delusions. It is the idea, put simply, that we are not our suffering.

Notably, lotus symbolism varies among different religious and cultural contexts. While it is commonly associated with Buddhism, it is also found in Hinduism, Jainism, and other spiritual traditions. The lotus's significance as a symbol of enlightenment resonates alongside its qualities of growth, purity, non-attachment, and beauty.

Moreover, the impermanence of time and the purity of a lotus have much to teach us about empathy and compassion. When we recognize the transient nature of our existence and time's limitation to Earth, we gain understanding of others' struggles, tame our personal suffering and continuous desires, expand our consciousness, and value interconnected contributions to our existence. We can *choose* to be inspired by another's victory or their service to others—and to make a difference in the worlds we create and the back yards we know and till—our own! Alternatively, some people who barely touch awareness also *choose* to wallow in the suffering of their perceptions, or become addicted to woes, or chain themselves to negative thought patterns and habitual behaviors, only to get lost in a vicious cycle of non-healing and never-ending psychosomatic ailments.

Consider, human beings take the same muddied journey through sentient life as the lotus, and this requires time—for ourselves and for others. But we each manage time differently. Every one of us dances to the rhythm of time's allotment to each of us—some faster and some more slowly. But time's impermanence is also a great equalizer. If we are fortunate enough to live, regardless of wealth, status, power, or influence, we are all, at least on this planet, gifted the same twenty-four-hour day. It is how we use this great gift that shapes our destiny, impacts the world, and bestows our legacy as stewards of the planet or others, our lives, and by extension, the cosmos.

TIME AS AN AGENT OF CHANGE

Instead of fearing or rushing through time's impermanence, give it a hug. I stop hurrying sometimes to hug trees, especially my Poinciana. I make time to *feel* the life within a plant and expect it to embrace me back, depositing sparks of energy into my being. You too, can relish time's transformative power. You don't have to hug trees if you find that a sappy thing to do (pun intended). But if the concept of time must imbue your life with a sense of angst, material success, and urgency, let it also offer you love, purpose, and peace. Understand that each passing second is indeed a ticking countdown to our transition through death, but it's also an invitation for growth, a canvas for creation, and a steppingstone on the path to revealing the enlightened phenomenal being within you, before you earn a tombstone!

Remember, the sunrise of each new day is a testament to life's indefatigable capacity for reinvention and renewal. A sunset too, is a poignant reminder of the transformation and beauty that can be found in endings. Amidst this ebb and flow, why not live, love, and learn with fervor and joy, but also with all the rest, peace, and reflection you're able to master?

Our lives are but a tiny seed in the expansive panorama we call existence, a fleeting lotus that begins life beneath the mud, but with time and our choices, reaches through darkness to transform into something glorious to behold.

Love – Life's Compass

"Your task is not to seek for love, but merely to seek and find all the barriers within yourself that you have built against it."
——Rumi

The archetypal, albeit unfortunate, modern American love story often unfolds as follows: We grow up, fall in love, marry, divorce, and the cycle repeats. Occasionally, children are involved, and tragically, some parents disappear from their offspring's lives once the marital bond is severed. This narrative isn't alien to me. I am a byproduct of divorce. My mother had an affair while married and presented me as the child of another man. Too young to comprehend the heated arguments or my sudden shift into foster care, I harbored an irrational guilt, erroneously believing their failures were somehow my fault.

In the court's care, I was reduced to a case number, devoid of guidance or stability but often lavished with unkind labels. Additionally, unexpected, and sudden relocations to new foster homes or schools left me perpetually uneasy and insecure, and feeling like an unwelcome burden to relatives. Being unmoored and adrift instilled in me little confidence, accountability, or an understanding of the value of relationships. Countless times I was silenced and reminded as a child of how *lucky* I was to receive a meal or a bed. Amid this emotional neglect, and loneliness, I learned to suppress my feelings. If tears escaped, they were met with hostility, so I learned to shut them down. Added to this fearful upbringing was a barrage of adult commentary lamenting my unfortunate circumstances as a foster kid and my pending dysfunctionality, "just like your mother."

Children are sponges for language and labels, and often lack the sophistication to process negative feedback or abusive situations. The outcomes can be traumatic. As I grew older, I found solace in drugs and alcohol. It masked my pain and prevented me from having to confront a person I didn't like very much —*me!* I fell in love easily and fell out even faster. I lived mostly detached, learning to shut off my emotions like a faucet. My personality was shaped by impulsiveness, sensitivity, lies, and a serious lack of self-awareness. I always braced for the inevitable abandonment, so I learned to "bite first." I've been divorced twice, married thrice, and parented four children by three different fathers, a pattern I finally, as an adult, resolved to break. Understanding why love was so fleeting for me required a deep exploration of self.

Interestingly, I maintained handwritten journals throughout my second, decade-long marriage (the first was right out of high school and barely lasted a year). Upon revisiting these entries, it's clear when and how this second marriage derailed. It began with nocturnal phone calls from strangers informing me about my husband's affairs. His lies about non-existent meetings were exposed when I covertly discovered his presence at an ex-lover's home. His friendships with women morphed into sexual relations, even after introducing me to them and expecting me to befriend them.

He insisted that marriage was about male dominance rather

than partnership. He said he loathed the mundane aspects of child rearing and that the person who had more experience in life should "wear the pants" and have the final word on important decisions. If he brought in the money, he said, he felt entitled to his whims. Instead of voicing my objections, I recoiled in silence, feeling betrayed and inferior. "But I have financial security," I told myself. "This is what men do, they cheat—and it's likely my fault, because I'm not ______________ (fill in the blank)." I reverted to childhood coping mechanisms. I shut down and tried to stay out of his way. I stuffed my suffering and hurt beneath a superficial perfect wife persona to keep the peace. The cognitive dissonance I experienced was excruciating.

My attempts to hold onto my husband's affection through outrageous lies and actions proved fruitless. My own indiscretions ensued as I sought validation elsewhere. A festering pool of distrust and resentment on both sides eventually made reconciliation impossible. Each of us had entered this relationship with unhealed emotional wounds and took up hard positions in separate trenches, readying for post-matrimonial battle. He was haunted by a previous marriage filled with belittlement and once had a challenging relationship with an overbearing father. He tried to tell me *before* we married that he was "self-centered, self-serving, and egotistical" (his words). I *chose* not to listen, thinking I could change him—and he likely assumed I'd acquiesce post-nuptial and "fall in line."

Despite my ex's tough exterior and harsh criticisms, I knew he harbored deep sensitivity, unresolved hurts and possessed a capacity for great love. I speculate he was afraid, as I was, to dive below the superficial surface of feelings to explore true intimacy and partnership. Control was easier for him than partnership because it was habitual and likely, comfortable. Passivity was my 'go to' because it was habitual and safe, even if uncomfortable. We both brought heavy baggage and distrust into our marriage and too often hid behind it. A smart man, my ex-husband was a perfectionist by many standards. People often turned to him for financial help or business advice—which he freely gave. Initially, we could talk for hours on a myriad of subjects. Later in the relationship, each of us inflicted deep wounds on the other. Instead of offering compassion, tolerance, discussion, or forgiveness, we engaged in a futile competition of criticism to prove who was the lesser culprit. We mostly overlooked the fact that we had intelligent, beautiful children together.

Our children were the ones who reminded me of the boundless and forgiving nature of love. As they grew, bearing witness to our mutual bitterness, they reached their limit. They declared their love for both of us, refusing to take sides. Their ***only*** choice was to choose love.

Therapy, embarked upon pre- and post-divorce, revealed hard and painful truths about me. While I confronted my flaws, I also discovered my capacity for resilience and healing, among them a healthy capability to love and form intimate connections.

Decades later, I am happily married to a wonderful man, and we've been together for seventeen years. Sometimes our marriage is a fireworks-loaded fairytale, but mostly it is a serene and valuable partnership filled with genuine love and intimacy.

Defining love: its power and necessity

The Essence of Love

From the dawn of time, humanity has endeavored to understand the true nature of love. Poets, philosophers, and scholars alike have wrestled with defining love in its myriad forms. It is a concept as vast as the cosmos, deeper than the Mariana Trench, and as complex as the human mind. Yet, despite love's indefinable complexities, it is universal. It exists as a fundamental force that drives us, shapes us, and, ultimately, defines us.

Love is an emotion, a connection, a commitment, a selfless act of giving without expecting anything in return. Love doesn't keep score. Love doesn't abuse. Love isn't about control or criticism or possession. It is a transformative force that pushes us to embrace vulnerability and lay down our weapons of arrogance, ego, and pride. Above all, love is "inner energy" others feel. It bonds us to others and encourages an extension of compassion, service, and kindness.

The Power of Love

Love is also a force that can make or break nations, heal, or wound hearts, and inspire or deter us. Love pushes us to be conscious in the moment...the *NOW*...to *inter-be* (as an enlightened monk once said) and feel emotion down to the very core of our being. Love, for better or worse, changes lives and, indeed, the world. Love is both bridge and blanket, sword, and swan, able to join forces and create changes that withstand tests of time and tragedy. And it can be downright frightening in its vulnerability if we're still running on outdated or primitive cognitive programming.

When authentically channeled, love has the capacity to heal old wounds and mend broken hearts. It can fill voids in our lives, provide comfort during times of sadness, and bring peace amidst turmoil. Love offers us courage in the face of fear, strength during adversity, and sprinkles hope over despair.

Love is more than grand gestures, epic wars, or fairytales. It's about the little things—shared laughter, mutual respect, moments of silence, a hug, the simple act of holding hands—and at times, even a heated argument rooted in sincere caring. It's about seeing and accepting other people in their entirety—their strengths and weaknesses, their triumphs, and failures—and still ***choosing*** to love them. It is about knowing when to hang on for life—and when to "let go" and "let be."

Meeting David

Years ago, in the sunlit corners of Naples, Florida, I clinked happy hour glasses with friends when I saw him, my future and final husband. It was a moment as electrifying as a bolt of lightning. I could barely muster the courage to speak to him and whispered to my friends, "That's it, I'm finished. I'm going to marry that man." The prophecy came true, but not before a personal tempest nearly capsized us. And, I will add, what I experienced when I first laid eyes on David, was *not* love but emotional intensity. I knew nothing about him. For all I knew at the time, I could have been repeating a familiar narrative, again choosing to "go after" someone in conquest fashion rather than to allow friendship to unfold—to blossom from mud to sun.

Unfortunately, and true to former form, a few months into our budding relationship, old tendencies surfaced. My unfounded fears gave birth to distrust. I unconsciously set traps for David, designing relationship trials, based on my insecurities, he was bound to fail. In the heat of one ugly argument, I screamed, "Get the fuck out of *my* house!"

I never anticipated that he would do just that.

My expectations were shattered. I anticipated him begging for mercy and permission to stay. Instead, he quietly and calmly collected his belongings and made his exit, not once looking back. I had meant to gain control, not lose him. My victory tasted bitter, leaving me heartbroken.

Days turned into a bleak marathon of weeks as I stared at my smartphone, hoping for a message but too fearful of rejection and full of pride to call him. Meanwhile, my friends bore the brunt of my desolation, listening to my laments. Then, like the first raindrop after a long drought, a single text from him lit up my screen: "*Hi.*"

David's message sparked hope. He wanted to talk. I had reservations about this. Within the battered baggage of my past, "talk" usually meant I'd be on the receiving end of a lecture, abuse, or a belittling remark—and rerouted to acquiesce to my partner's demands. But David was different. He wanted us to lay down some rules before we talked, to help foster respect and understanding, to keep our disagreements from escalating into a storm: 1. No name-calling 2. No shouting and 3. Nobody can leave until the issue is resolved.

This form of communication was completely new territory for me. It's one thing to sit in a therapist's office baring your soul on your best behavior but quite another to implement logical coping and communication strategies in the face of passion!

As I arrived at his place, my heart involuntarily prepared for a battlefield. Instead, I walked into a haven. A delicious dinner was spread, candles flickered, and the fragrance of flowers filled the air. David took time to set the space. He cared. No man before him had ever put in so much effort to prioritize *love* above *sex*. But most surprising was the sight of David, my stalwart man, with red-rimmed eyes. He was brave enough to reveal selfless vulnerability. And it has been the *consistency* of this love, rather than its *intensity* that has taught me more about intimacy and partnership than I ever dreamed possible.

David is a man of strength, and by completely unfair stereotypical standards, he's considered an "alpha" male. He's worked as a police officer, was a hunter, a college baseball pitcher, and a vice president of sales for a start-up technology company. Yet before me stood a man shedding his walls, displaying raw emotions. It was an eye-opener, showing me that our somewhat new relationship was not a game of control or conquest to him but had real partnership potential. We'd have to *choose* to work together—to be a team.

Trust between us didn't bloom overnight, but slowly and steadily. I started to understand the profound worth of intimacy found in authentic love, all thanks to the lessons David's resilience, gentleness, and strength imparted. His humility, support, encouragement, and loyalty continue to guide me, paving our path to a once-in-a-lifetime love that daily deepens.

. . .

The Necessity of Love

Love is a necessity for human beings. We are wired for connection, intimacy, shared experiences, and being seen, accepted, and understood. Without love, we become rickety boats adrift on a vast ocean, taking on the poisoned waters of stress, ennui, and sadness, feeling aimless and lost. Love provides an anchor, one that stabilizes our senses and our being. It also provides a compass to guide our hearts toward empathy and understanding.

Love nurtures souls and fuels connection. It supports mental, emotional, and psychological health. It provides a sense of belonging, purpose, and peace. While it may be true that humans (and animals) can *survive* without love, they rarely (if ever) *thrive* in its absence. Love is necessary for personal fulfillment and vital for societal harmony. Love fosters compassion, understanding, and tolerance—values that are fundamental to the existence of a peaceful planet. And Love appears to us in many forms.

Love, an Ongoing Journey

Defining love is difficult, I think, because it's complex and dynamic. It incorporates and reflects the unique perceptions and experiences of every individual. And so, as we journey through life, our understanding of love constantly evolves depending on our nature, our environment, and the nurturing we get and give.

In its essence, love is a lifelong personal trip to self-understanding. It's an adventure too, filled at times with challenge and hardship. Yet it is through love that we weather trials and tribulations. And as we navigate the sometimes-icy journey of mismatched relationships, let us remember that love, in all its forms, is a gift of warmth and light—one that is free to both give and receive—and this includes learning to love yourself despite encountering a few rejections, 'get the fuck outs', or lies along the way. Alternatively, we must also develop the courage to leave when a relationship is too dangerous to stay. So, spread the love, whenever and wherever you're able! Think about this: What's the alternative?

The role of love in personal growth

Love plays a significant role in human personal growth. It has a profound impact on an individual's emotional, psychological, and social development when freely given or purposely withheld.

It's important to note that love alone does not *guarantee* personal growth. Personal growth also requires self-reflection and a willingness to engage in personal development. This can be, at least initially, emotionally painful hard work. We must reopen and confront the old wounds found deep in our cells, clean them, and allow them to metabolize out of our system using forgiveness, compassion, and reframing. Love is a powerful catalyst for these potions and a nurturing force capable of blunting past injuries.

Love as a guiding force

In the era of Covid-19, I found remote working purpose in assisting businesses to develop safety protocols and re-opening guidelines. Among the countless lives impacted by the pandemic were Mike and Ilene, proud owners of a successful property management company in Arizona.

To express their gratitude, Mike extended an unexpected invitation for a two-week stay at one of their heavenly homes in Sedona. We leaped at the chance, selecting a grand five-bedroom mansion, intending to share our good fortune with friends. But fate had other plans; work obligations held our friends to jobs, and we found ourselves journeying alone to the mesmerizing area, a land previously untouched by our footsteps.

Following a delightful evening in Phoenix, we embarked on our three-hour ride toward the majestic red rocks of Sedona. My first glimpse of the towering geological wonders shook me to my core; I was consumed by a wave of emotion so powerful, I sobbed. There was an energy here, an energy that enveloped us, beckoning us into its embrace. And I felt so much love.

The house was perched at the apex of a mountain and offered a panorama of nature's beauty. It also, we learned, served as an abode for Native American Shaman retreats. One night, under the star-studded canopy, I felt a profound yearning. I turned to my husband, and the words tumbled out with unexpected certainty, "Tomorrow, I need to meet a man with a flute."

Bemused, David laughed, assuming the comment was spurred by copious wine consumption. The next morning, we hiked to the famous Boynton Vortex, a local landmark known for special energies. On a nearby peak, a man was in deep conversation with another couple.

As he neared us, I exclaimed, "It's the man with the flute!"

My husband looked puzzled. "I don't see any flute!"

I ran to this stranger, forgetting I was a grown woman, now engrossed with all the wonder, immaturity, and naiveté of a child at play.

The man smiled and graciously introduced himself. He suggested we sit on a ledge overlooking the majestic valley to share conversation. I'd have to climb—high. I was terrified of heights. With the man's encouragement, I made the trek. For the next three hours, Johnny and I delved into profound topics that danced between the supernatural and scientific realms. The heart of our discourse, however, centered on the immense importance of Love.

In a magical twist, he produced a wooden flute from his

pocket and began to play, fulfilling my seemingly nonsensical prophecy. Another man suddenly poked his head into our ledge, adding to the surreal nature of the moment. He thrust a heart-shaped rock into my palm and with a deep, resonating voice stated, "The most important thing to do in life is **LOVE**!" He smiled widely, clambered over our heads, and joined the original flute player in a hauntingly beautiful duet.

In that instant, beneath the infinite sky, between two flute-playing strangers, amidst the mesmerizing red rocks, I found myself part of a tale that was both strange and wondrous. It was a tale that echoed through time, the strength of connections, the power of prophecy, and above all, the profound importance of love.

Love's guiding role is exemplified through its power to catalyze social change.

History is abundant with stories of people driven by love to combat injustice, fight for freedom, and strive for equality. The Civil Rights Movement, the Suffragette Movement, The LGBTQ+ Movement, Honoring Fallen Soldiers & Veterans, and more recently, the fight for human rights around the globe, and helping one another through the last pandemic. All tragedies and some wars are driven by a profound sense of love for fellow human beings, and a yearning for a fair, just world. Love, in these instances, becomes a superpower of consciousness that propels individuals and communities to stand against oppression or violence and to foster grand social transformation.

Rumi was a soul driven by love. He was a 13th-century Persian poet and theologian. Rumi's poetry centers on themes of love, mystical exploration, friendship, and ecstatic identification with the divine. His works are sincere and intense as they encapsulate the paradigms of Sufi philosophy and a quest for sublime awareness *of* and a personal relationship *with* God.

Rumi was born in 1207 in the Persian Empire, some say in the city of Balkh (in modern-day Afghanistan) or Vakhsh (now in Tajikistan). Due to the Mongol invasions, his family moved westward, traveling through Baghdad, Mecca, and Damascus, before finally settling in Konya, in present-day Turkey. His life changed dramatically in 1244 when he met a wandering dervish (one who practices austerity and love) named Shams Tabrizi (Shining Light or Son of Light). Shams was often disparaged by Islamic clerics because he had the courage to call them out when they forbade women to seek God in the mosque, or adorned themselves with fur and gold, and then claimed it was only through a cleric that one could commune with God. This meeting with Shams was a central event in Rumi's life, leading to a profound friendship and spiritual deepening that inspired much of his poetry. Rumi put out a call to action for kindness and compassion is rooted in love, regardless of race, creed, color, sex, gender, religion, or ethnicity.

Rumi's influence continues today, and his poetry is appreciated for its depth and beauty, touching on the universal human experience and the quest for a meaningful life. His works have been widely translated and interpreted in various forms, including music, dance (most notably the whirling dervishes), and other art forms.

As Rumi reminds us, love extends beyond interpersonal relationships and societal actions. It is also found in the realms of creativity and innovation. Many of the world's greatest artworks, literary pieces, and musical compositions have been inspired by love, bearing testament to its profound influence on our lives. Love for knowledge and understanding guides scientists, researchers, poets, writers, artists, and scholars, fueling human engines of progress and innovation.

Love is also so much more than sentiment. It is an impetus that guides our actions and influences our choices. It shapes our relationships, motivates our ambitions, and drives social change. By embracing love as a guide, you cultivate a world that values unity, fosters empathy, and promotes growth—and in many instances, steers you around harm's way or plays a great part in making a positive difference in another's life. It is through this perspective of love that we appreciate its role as a powerful compass on our voyage of human existence.

Compassion & Empathy

In the heart of San Jose, Costa Rica, I found myself at the Hotel Del Ray, linked to the thriving Blue Marlin Bar and Casino. Years ago, I undertook a research project on the local and legal prostitution industry. As Saturday night descended, the front of the house sparkled with vibrant lights and echoing chatter, gamblers enthralled in competing waves of exhilaration and loss.

A dimmer ambiance took over the back area, a separate pub-like space where American men sought purely physical amusement from an array of women available for purchase at the bar, women lined up in multi-colored pastel halter tops, which included, curiously, Russian nationals. My bodyguard, a towering figure who had mastered English from Tom Hanks movies, navigated me through the throng. Some say my non-judgmental attitude and compassion invite openness to this sort of thing, but divinely inspired curiosity, I believe, is my true ally.

Prostitution is lawful in Costa Rica, and brothels dot the landscape from San Jose to Jaco La Playa. The women I conversed with were mostly career sex-workers, a strictly personal choice made from socio-economic constraints, at peace with their profession and puzzled by Americans' discomfort with the exchange of money for sexual pleasure. As one woman remarked, she didn't need *saving* as much as she hoped for *authenticity.* Midnight marked the end of my interviews, and we trod our path out through casino hurdles, into a carnival atmosphere.

The streets were alive with performers and vagabonds, some brewing coffee in rusty carts or immersed in card games. Amidst the chaos, a young boy, about eight, caught my attention. He stared vacantly through me, gnawing a Styrofoam cup, dirt clinging to his hair and fingernails. As he approached, Tony abruptly shoved him away, ushering me into the van. After a swift reprimand to the boy, Tony slid into the driver's seat.

His actions left me seething, "Why? Why would you hit a child?" I protested.

"Because he will rob you, that's why! The boy is addicted to glue!" Tony responded, followed by a cynical laugh about the boy's parental void. He swept his hand across the windshield. "They're all high, these kids." And that's when I saw them—about twenty homeless kids in various states of despair, going ignored by throngs of tourists. Tony's words stung, the street kids' plight unfurling before my eyes. "You think this is bad...let me show you something."

Tony then drove me to a desolate part of town. As we arrived at a dim intersection, he shouted into the darkness, receiving a frail reply. A small figure emerged, a barefooted girl in an oversized ragged dress. Her request for a "gift," someone to have sex with, left me recoiling with disgust. How could anyone sexually abuse a *child*?

"Put her in the van," I said to Tony.

He vehemently refused. "She belongs to a gang guy I know. We can't take her with us."

"Call the police," I said.

"The police are corrupt and on the guy's payroll," he answered.

An argument ensued about *our* possible arrest if we put her in the van and were ourselves accused of kidnapping, and the terrifying prospect of a night in a Costa Rican jail. Our argument ended with me conceding to Tony's logic, but pissed at him too, for his seeming heartlessness. I felt helpless. I had kids at home snug in their beds, protected from such harsh cruelties. If it's not impossible, there must be a way to get her out of here, I thought. But when you're angry or emotional, I've also learned, you're not typically lucid.

I named the girl *Emma* because she refused to tell us her name. I reached into my purse and handed her all the money I had, enough Tony said, to buy her a couple of days' respite. It was all I could do. I returned to the hotel, grief-stricken and feeling guilty.

Two nights later, I revisited that crumbling and desolate corner accompanied by others who might be able to help. Emma was nowhere to be found. I never saw her again, but I never forgot her either. She was the girl, for me, who wasn't saved.

As humans, sometimes all we can offer at a moment's notice is compassion. I yearned to gather Emma and these other street kids together like a bushel of apples; to cut away the rotten parts of their lives and polish each one anew, to heal their wounds and give them a fresh start. But I knew I couldn't do it alone. I needed love, money, and a miracle.

Understanding—no—*feeling* the world through another's suffering is not a distant and detached cognitive exercise. It is a cornerstone of love. I tried to truly imagine what it must be like for Emma—alone, on the streets, being sexually assaulted and abused by multiple strangers night after night. How did she blunt the horror of the crimes committed against her? Could she? And—would she ever be okay?

Compassion and empathy, at their essence, form the foundational blocks of our social fabric. Compassion, derived from the Latin root meaning "to suffer with," is an emotional perception of another's suffering. It involves an authentic desire to help. It's an altruistic attribute that propels us to act selflessly to ease the pain of others. It comes in many forms such as holding a person's hand at their hour of death, deep listening, sending flowers, buying groceries, or fundraising for disaster-stricken regions. Compassion bounces positive energy into our daily lives and shapes us into elevated benevolent beings.

Empathy, by comparison, is an ability to understand and share the feelings of another. It is often described as "walking in someone else's shoes" (even if they wear none), allowing us to perceive the world from their perspective. Empathy goes beyond understanding; it involves sharing another's emotional experience, a crucial aspect in building genuine connections.

The interplay between compassion and empathy is profound. It allows us to recognize and understand another's feelings, creating a sense of shared experience. Compassion takes this shared understanding further, inspiring us to act upon these feelings and alleviate distress—to interconnect with another and the world. It is this interconnectedness that makes these virtues, empathy, and compassion, vital cornerstones of love.

In a world pockmarked by vitriol, materialism, corruption, conflict, and misunderstanding, I firmly feel that the need for empathy and compassion is necessary. Most of us have veiled our hearts to the potency of each. As society grapples with issues like human trafficking, war, racial or gender inequality, starvation, political polarization, pandemics, pollution, or social injustices; compassion, and empathy have the capacity to foster peace, unity, and reconciliation—to bring us closer, and to realize that we are more alike in our expectations of safety, shelter, security, health, and love, than we realize.

In the realm of personal relationships, these virtues are equally paramount. They enable us to forge deeper connections, promote emotional well-being, and cultivate an environment of mutual respect, love, and understanding. Whether it's in the comforting silence shared with a grieving friend or the joyful celebration of a loved one's success, empathy and compassion are inextricably woven into our lives and experiences.

Nurturing compassion and empathy requires introspection

and practice. It also calls for openness, a willingness to embrace vulnerability, nonjudgment, and the courage to step outside of our comfort zones. In doing so, we expand our understanding, challenge our biases, and invite possibility—to create peaceful environments where compassion, great ideas, and empathy thrive. People are disarmed by genuine acts of kindness.

Though I couldn't save Emma, the empathy and compassion her plight ignited within me set me on a lifelong mission to rescue children like her. In her own distinct way, Emma made an indelible impact and forged a connection with me that I'll forever cherish. Her eyes, dull with despair and trapped in a world she didn't understand, were what drew me to her. Emma's tragic reality shook me to my core. I couldn't ignore her haunting image; couldn't turn away.

In a world too often filled with darkness, Emma's story was my personal call to action rooted in love. I'm no police officer or superhero able to swoop in and save the day, but I have something else, something possibly even more powerful: a pen, a voice, and a unique set of skills as a former foster kid, psychiatric assessment specialist, and advocate.

Determined to make a difference, I began researching human trafficking. I had to learn who and what the enemy was before I could enter combat. I reached out to organizations dedicated to rescuing others. I talked with attorneys, federal agents, social workers, undercover operators, and victim assistance specialists. I realized that through the power of words, I could educate others and help both private and public sector entities in formulating effective strategies, programs, and policies to combat this terrifying crime.

I realized that realism and circumspection were vital, but I was also driven by immense compassion to speak for those whose voices, bodies, and freedoms were stolen from them. I decided I would highlight the horrors faced by these innocent souls and share what concerned parties can do to help them.

But I didn't stop there.

Working closely with public and private agencies, academics, and nonprofit organizations, I began to delve into the minds of traffickers, most of them like their victims in terms of prior trauma, abuse, suffering and survival—but quite different in their levels of dehumanization and violence. My insights helped in understanding the trafficker mind, providing valuable information that led to a few successful rescues.

As I immersed myself in this tragic world, the memory of Emma's eyes never left me. It is a reminder of why I do this. She is also my symbol of hope that others similarly situated will be rescued, their lives healed and rebuilt upon foundations of love and care. I have played a modest role in this battle for salvation, a role that I must humbly acknowledge is challenging to take true credit for. I'm acutely aware of how many others have delved far deeper into the trenches of human trafficking, making immense personal sacrifices to save lives, and their efforts far overshadow my limited contribution. These are the brave souls in national security who remain behind-the-scenes not wanting or expecting thanks, awards, or accolades.

My fingertips guide my heart to create stories that may help draw Emma and others out of the darkness of slavery and into the saving light of love. In our stories, I found my purpose, my part in a bigger picture, a testament to the fact that anyone, no matter their profession or skills, can make a measurable difference in the lives of others. All it takes is the courage to care and the will to act.

Selflessness v. Passivity

Selflessness and passivity are two attributes often used to describe individuals and their interactions with others on a path to love. While there may be superficial similarities, a more in-depth examination reveals stark differences between the two. To fully understand these differences, it is essential to define what each entail.

Selflessness refers to a character trait characterized by a high degree of altruism and benevolence, where an individual routinely puts the needs and interests of others ahead of his or her own without playing the part of a martyr or expecting something in return. This act of placing others first includes charity, volunteering, or making personal sacrifices for the benefit of others. This trait is largely applauded and admired in society as it is often synonymous with sincerity and kindness.

Conversely, passivity involves a lack of assertiveness. It may manifest as aggressive inaction or submission to the will of others, regardless of the individual's personal needs or interests. Unlike selflessness, passivity usually stems from a fear of confrontation, lack of self-esteem, or avoidance of responsibility. While selflessness is an active choice, passivity is more often a reactive stance with roots in survival or trauma.

The key difference between selflessness and passivity lies in the motive and outcome of the actions. Selflessness is driven by empathy, compassion, and a genuine desire to enhance the well-being of others without seeking applause, accolades, awards, or credit. It is often accompanied by a sense of fulfillment and satisfaction, leading to positive self-esteem and healthy interpersonal relationships. It involves willingly making sacrifices, having carefully *evaluated* choices, and opting for a path that benefits a greater good over self-aggrandizement.

Conversely, passivity springs from a different set of motivations, often rooted in avoiding conflict or asserting oneself due to fear or a lack of confidence. A passive nature often leads to suppressed feelings, resentment, and a lack of personal growth. Passive individuals mostly choose to neglect their needs because they find it challenging and fearful to assert their needs. Or they may believe themselves unworthy of having their needs met, typically due to unresolved childhood trauma and/or abuse.

Alternatively, passive individuals typically find themselves frequently disadvantaged or exploited. As they struggle to express their wants or needs, they inadvertently enable others to disregard their welfare due to the type of physical and mental energy they exchange in their environment. This can lead to feelings of resentment, denial, guilt, shame, humiliation, dissatisfaction, paranoia, suspicion, or distrust. This passivity fosters an atmosphere of energy that envelops hurting souls into a repeated cycle of negative habits. But once we understand and admit our fears, it is possible to overcome them through building a sturdier base of new habits. Then we can discard the weak scaffolding of any wobbly inner constructs that fail to strengthen our resolve.

Long term, selflessness and passivity yield different outcomes. Selfless individuals, due to their proactive concern for others, positively impact their surroundings, are a joy to be around, and establish harmonious relationships because they have no hidden or nefarious agendas. Their actions are often met with gratitude, respect, and reciprocation, promoting a nurturing and supportive environment.

While both selflessness and passivity may appear similar because each involves putting others' needs first, their motivations and consequences differentiate them. As individuals navigate interpersonal relationships, understanding these differences leads to healthier communication and a more authentic expression of self.

If you find yourself on the passive side of life, as I once was, here are some suggestions:

- **Be kind to yourself.** Just as you would express concern or empathy toward a friend, do so for you. Start a private prayer or conversation by expressing genuine concern for your well-being. Listen to and support the inner idea that people care for you. If needed, seek out a trusted friend or family member to talk with.

• **Banish the Critic in your Head:** While it's completely normal to occasionally berate yourself, it's detrimental if such thoughts dominate your existence. Negative self-talk has a profound impact on our success, outlook, health, and even the partners or friendships we choose. When we lock up our brains within the constraints of adverse babble, say, reliving a fight or mentally abusing ourselves (i.e., *"I'm such a dumbass." "People hate me." "I'm an idiot!")*, we push our own self-destruct buttons. This turns up the volume of our internal fight-or-flight response and raises stress. Constantly setting your mind to negative internal static stimulates repeated problems and the continuation of negative habit patterns. This breeds a ripple effect of dysfunctional coping skills, chronic health issues and/or poor behavioral choices.

• **Validate your feelings**: Recognize and validate your emotions without judgment. Your feelings and experiences *are* genuine, even if they sometimes lie outside the boundaries of being valid. You're not alone. It's completely understandable that you might feel angry, trapped, or unsure, and it's important to acknowledge your feelings, accept them, and then discover positive people or activities that propel you toward peace. If your feelings seem too much to manage during a high-stress event, disengage if you're able. If you feel you may harm yourself or others, again, please seek professional help.

• **Practice combat breathing**: Soldiers and Marines often learn a breathing technique called "box breathing" or "combat breathing," which involves inhaling, holding the breath, exhaling, and holding again, each step for a count of four. This technique is commonly used to help manage anxiety and regulate emotions during high-stress situations or combat scenarios. Here's a breakdown of the technique:

Inhale: Take a slow, deep breath through the nose, counting to four. Fill your lungs completely with air, allowing your abdomen and chest to rise.
Hold: Hold your breath for a count of four. Keep your lungs filled with air and maintain a relaxed state.
Exhale: Exhale slowly through the mouth, counting to four. Empty your lungs completely, allowing your abdomen and chest to relax.
Hold: Hold your breath again for a count of four. Maintain a state of relaxation without any air in your lungs.
Repeat: After the fourth step, repeat the cycle by inhaling again and continuing the pattern for several minutes or until a sense of calmness and control is achieved.

Combat breathing, as I learned in a certified *Stop the Bleed* Class, is considered effective because it activates the parasympathetic nervous system, which promotes relaxation and counteracts the fight-or-flight response triggered during stressful situations. By practicing this technique regularly, soldiers develop a valuable self-regulation skill that is beneficial in managing intense pressure situations and reestablishing personal control.

- **Encourage yourself**: Share experiences or feelings, as you feel comfortable, without fear of judgment. Create a safe space to express feelings openly, knowing that you are there to listen, learn, and support yourself into healing—even if this requires writing in a journal, safely venting, or sobbing into a pillow.

• **Mentally highlight your strengths and agency**: Recognize your inner strength and empower yourself to make decisions. Remember those moments when someone thanked you or complimented something about you, or when you accomplished a new task, learned a new skill, or helped someone. You can create positive change in your life but must believe in your capacity to do so.

• **Seek information and resources**: Research available resources, such as helplines, support groups, alternative therapies, or counseling services. If applicable to your situation, seek professional help from organizations that specialize in supporting individuals with addiction issues or in abusive relationships.

• **Avoid pushy or pressuring people**: While it's important to receive support and encouragement on your transformative safari, it's also crucial for you to respect your need for autonomy. Avoid being pressured into making decisions or taking actions that discomfort you and your spirit. You are in control of your choices and how you react to your circumstances. And sometimes good choices require severing old ties or habits and haunts that no longer serve your mental, emotional, or spiritual health.

• **Fly Away:** Remember too, it's essential to approach yourself with empathy, patience, and understanding—sometimes self-love and growth require flying away from those who deplete or dim your inner light—even if the only flight you can take is inward.

Emptiness – A Canvas for Creation

Once I knew only darkness and stillness... my life was without past or future... but a little word from the fingers of another fell into my hand that clutched at emptiness, and my heart leaped to the rapture of living."
—Helen Keller

Years ago, I crossed paths with an extraordinary individual. He was a colleague and mentor who won my admiration despite his sometimes-gruff exterior and penchant for bending the rules. Neil C. was his name, a man hailing from the humble origins of inner-city Cleveland, Ohio. Neil sculpted his destiny into a monument of success. Beginning as a robust high school football player, he navigated life's hurdles to emerge as a college graduate. His journey did not stop there; his grit, resilience, and indomitable spirit propelled him to become one of Ohio's most influential "super lobbyists." By all appearances, his life was a testament to the unyielding will of the human spirit.

The tale of Neil, however, took a tragic turn when I read one morning in a local paper that he'd committed suicide in a

Florida park. His sudden demise sent ripples of shock throughout the Ohio political landscape and beyond. He died, I later learned, during a tumultuous time in his life. He was embroiled in a federal racketeering charge related to an alleged bribery scheme. The case revolved around a $1 billion bailout for two nuclear plants in northern Ohio, both places where my grandfather had once worked. Despite pleading not guilty, the pressure bore heavily on Neil's shoulders—yet he never said a word to me. He even accompanied me to a local fundraiser for Florida's then-attorney general, putting me in the spotlight with elected officials as he remained quietly in the shadows, observant, insightful, and guiding.

The news of his passing shook the foundations of my world. To me, Neil was more than just a mentor; he was a friend. His burdens remained hidden behind his stubborn veil of stoicism, leaving me oblivious to the turmoil he battled. Even during our occasional conversations where I'd call to ask him about policy strategy, he kept his struggles secret. His sudden death filled me with profound sadness. But it also taught me a lesson about the difference between loss and emptiness.

Neil was a man of intellect, resilience, and despite his flaws (which we all have), a man of character. His love for family, friends, and his wife was evident, and so was the influence he had on many lives, including mine. It's hard for me to pinpoint where or *if* Neil faltered along the way, or whether he was just a pawn in someone else's game. In truth, it holds little relevance now. The dead are silent, and life continues its unyielding march forward, perhaps as Neil would have wanted—on his own terms.

His death serves as a reminder to me of the impermanence of life, urging us to cherish each moment, each relationship, and each struggle that shapes us—even in the face of emptiness—or perhaps, because of it. But Neil's death is also an opportunity for me to redefine *emptiness.* Experiences, whether we perceive them as good or bad, make us who we are, and it's the legacy we leave behind that truly matters.

Emptiness as a starting point, not an end

Emptiness.

Westerners often read or think about this word with a sense of fear or a feeling of dread, lack, and isolation. As a philosophical or existential concept, *emptiness* often resonates negative undertones if accompanied by "I feel empty" or "my life is void of meaning." However, emptiness, perhaps, should be celebrated and reframed because it offers us a chance at transformation. Rather than being a guilt-loaded grim ending, emptiness should be viewed as a starting point, a fresh canvas primed for narratives, explorations, and enlightenment. It is fertile ground for self-discovery and renewal. And a great motivator. It is the absence of what was or what could be, which is sometimes intimidating or tragic, but also inspiring. Emptiness is the space that grants us freedom to create and imagine without constraint.

In life, we pass through different phases, each accompanied by its unique set of experiences, emotions, challenges, triumphs, and perceptions. However, there is always a transitional period characterized by an "emptiness" before the commencement of each new phase. These periods of emptiness are significant junctures that allow us to shed old identities, reassess our perspectives, and clear the path for fresh possibilities. Emptiness doesn't have to be a tombstone, but rather, a stepping-off point.

Every time I finish writing a book, I feel empty for a while. After my first published work, I cried, thinking that I'd accomplished my goal and couldn't possibly come up with another unique idea to put to paper, let alone produce anything people might want to read! But sitting with my emptiness, I realized, helps me rest, and explore, before I pour new words onto blank paper. Emptiness forces me to climb new heights across vast expanses of nothing—to create—something!

In many instances, this existential vacuum is a catalyst for self-improvement and exploration. It prods us to evaluate our current circumstances. It invites us to redefine our perspectives, and ultimately propels us toward the stars. When we experience emptiness as a void instead of an opportunity, it is usually our subconscious mind highlighting an area in our lives requiring attention—likely something unresolved or left undone. Therefore, recognizing emptiness as a starting point might be the spark you need for all constructive systems within you to launch.

Emptiness and Personal Growth

Emptiness is a chance to question our narratives and the interpretations of our experiences, and in doing so, gain the capacity to rewire them. By making peace with emptiness, we become open to experience, to new levels of depth and understanding.

Emptiness and Mindfulness

Emptiness also serves as an opportunity to practice mindfulness, to sit with ourselves and acknowledge and accept our feelings without judgment. When we sit in our emptiness without trying to fill it in with random or negative thoughts, or escape from it by doing something, anything else, we begin to understand its nature and our reactions to it. Resting in emptiness brings clarity, patience, and compassion, enabling us to engage with life fully and authentically. And it isn't initially easy, especially for the fast-paced Western world.

In Zen philosophy, the concept of "empty mind" is central.

It is considered a state of openness, a readiness to receive the universe as it is, without preconceived notions or judgments. This state of mind is a starting point for many to emotional intelligence, spiritual growth, and self-actualization, the trifecta of enlightenment.

Emptiness, therefore, is not an end; it is a mechanism of evolution. It allows us to step away from our habitual perceptions and enables us to see new paths and possibilities. It does not mean embracing desolation, death, or nothingness. Instead, it's an opportunity to shape and fill our internal and external spaces with fresh experiences and wisdom. Life, therefore, does not end with emptiness; rather, it finds new beginnings here.

Embracing Emptiness as a Space for Possibility

Emptiness might also be perceived as a portal to creativity. Just as nature abhors a vacuum, the human psyche seeks to fill emptiness with something meaningful. This instinctual response stimulates imagination and encourages problem-solving, offering valuable opportunities for insight, internal journeys, and episodes of enlightenment.

Innovative ideas often emerge from this void because discomfort and fear sometimes accompany emptiness. Emptiness compels individuals to think beyond the tyranny of the left brain, to bypass conventional wisdom and venture into the uncharted territory of our vast floating minds. Thus, emptiness should not be viewed as an end or failure, but as a beginning—a fresh open space for new adventures.

Utilizing Emptiness as a Catalyst for Transformation

Transforming emptiness into an opportunity requires a shift in mindset. Instead of regarding emptiness as a void to be feared, we should see it as a challenge that fuels personal growth. When we harness the power of emptiness, we realize that it's not about escaping our feelings but leveraging them. It equips us with a more profound understanding of ourselves and the world around us.

In practical terms, emptiness can be converted into opportunity by investing in personal growth—learning new skills, pursuing passions, establishing meaningful relationships, or serving others. Emptiness is an integral part of the human condition just like fulfillment—consider them the bottom and top of a vase you may fill with whatever loosens your lotus! By reconfiguring our perception of emptiness, it becomes fertile ground for possibility rather than a frightening abyss.

Neil's suicide, as tragic as it was, did not happen in vain. While it left some of his cohorts feeling adrift and hollow for a while, me included, that void was quickly imbued with the enduring legacy he left behind. His teachings, his extraordinary talent, his unique sense of humor, and his insatiable desire to excel continue to inspire me, filling the emptiness he initially left behind with a sense of purpose and connection to his spirit.

The Power of Dreams

"Throw your dreams into space like a kite, and you do not know what it will bring back, a new life, a new friend, a new love, a new country."
—Anais Nin

One Ohio night in July, I found myself stirred from sleep. The exact hour eluded me, but an indefinable sound lured me awake. From my bed, I surveyed the scene outside the screen door, gazing into a world swathed in the monochrome hues of nighttime. The usual, reassuring forms of trees and bushes blurred into ghostly silhouettes appeared; the familiar sight of our patio transformed into an abstract tableau. All was *normal...*or so I thought.

Glancing toward my slumbering husband, I noticed his calm and deep breaths—unusual for him. He's startled by the slightest noise. I reached out and touched him; still, he remained undisturbed. Ensuring the sheet snugly enveloped him, I retreated to my pillow, my gaze settling on the alluring darkness outside the open French door.

I'm unsure how I wound up outside, dressed in my nightgown, in the heart of the valley beneath our home. Unexpectedly, I was not alone. Towering beside me was a humanoid figure—an extraterrestrial—radiating an ethereal glow. Yet, I felt no dread. Instead, a feeling of warmth and familiarity flooded me, as if I were reuniting with a long-lost companion. I knew, instinctively, that this entity was far superior to me in wisdom and spiritual development. Awestruck, I found myself communicating with him, not through words, but through the silent language of thoughts.

The moist grass beneath my feet and the summer air's intoxicating scent anchored me into this surreal experience. Finally, curiosity overtook me. "How do you travel here?" I asked.

"To help you comprehend," he replied, "I will use terms within your understanding." His arm, ending in four long digits but no thumb, extended, tracing a strange triangle filled with alien symbols in the air. On one of the slopes of the triangle, he etched a circle. "We slide along the slope of a perfect right triangle," he cryptically explained.

My confusion deepened. "I don't see a spaceship," I said, looking around.

His response was a nod, followed by an upward gesture.

My eyes followed his direction, scanning the trees and our home's silhouette beneath an expansive night sky. Suddenly, out of the blackness materialized a magnificent, gigantic spacecraft adorned with clear dazzling lights, like nothing I had ever imagined. Its size covered the entire length of our home and then some! The sight stole my breath, causing my knees to buckle. His reaction was a silent laugh, head tipped back, like a paternal chuckle at a child's innocent bewilderment.

But as swiftly as the strange unidentified object appeared, I found myself back in bed, my husband sleeping peacefully beside me. As I tried to comprehend the surreal episode, I was left pondering: Was this a fantastical dream embedded within another dream, or an actual cosmic encounter cleverly disguised as a dreamscape? The enigma lingered, leaving me both enchanted and puzzled as I ventured back into the realm of sleep, the memory of the alien's silent chuckle and warm eyes already making me miss my new-old extraterrestrial "friend."

Throughout the annals of human history, dreams have persistently served as potent forces, driving us beyond the threshold of the known into the realms of the undiscovered. The ethereal nature of dreams often intertwines with our aspirations, creating an intricate dance of possibility and desire that illuminates the pathways of our lives. As nocturnal narratives emerge from the depths of our subconscious minds, dreams encompass a world that defies the constraints of our earthly reality. They are mystical echoes of our innermost thoughts, fears, and desires, cloaked in an often-incomprehensible language of symbolism and metaphor. Dreams enable us to transcend the mundane and journey into the mystic, navigating the uncharted seas of our psyche. We become astral travelers and shamans taking supernatural tours who embark on mysterious adventures.

In esoteric form, dreams provide an invaluable platform for self-discovery and introspection. Each cryptic symbol or hidden metaphor uncovers latent truths about our being. Dreams reveal layers of our identity otherwise hidden by waking hours beneath a facade of consciousness. When we learn to decipher dream-encoded messages, we unlock facets of ourselves that remain obscured during our waking lives. Dreams, thus, serve as celestial lighthouses, guiding us through the murky waters of the unknown toward an enlightened understanding of our inner selves and of the cosmos of which we're a part.

On the other hand, daydreams, reasonably conscious fantasies about our hopes, fears, or aspirations, represent the dawn that follows the mystic night of dreaming. If nocturnal dreams are the silent whisperings of our subconscious mind, daydreams are the active voice of our conscious intent, where we are the directors and producers of its content. Daydreams represent various embers in our hearts. They draw us toward the future or keep us lingering in the past, but mostly dare us to envisage a reality beyond the immediacy of the present. Additionally, daydreams are more than mere wants, wishes, or fears; daydreams are aspirations deeply planted in the fertile soil of our beliefs. They can spur creativity, provide direction, and transform foggy vistas into navigable maps.

The symbiotic relationship between nightdreaming and daydreams is also a fascinating spectacle of human experience. While dreams help us delve into the profound depths of our subconscious selves, daydreams provide a semi-conscious, purposeful trajectory, pulling us forward into a future we yearn to create—or holding us to a past where perceived outcomes may hold us prisoner.

This profound dance between subconscious dreams and our conscious manipulation of daydreams, the inner self, and the outer world, shapes our human adventure. As we dream, we tap into the wellspring of our authentic selves, unearthing our deepest fears and desires. As we aspire in daydreams, we channel these insights into purposeful action, molding our reality to mirror the vision of our dreams.

Dreams and daydreams are essential elements of our human psyche. They bind together the esoteric and the pragmatic, the mystical and the tangible, the subconscious and the conscious, guiding us on our voyage through space and time. Understanding and honoring this powerful interplay allows us to navigate this world (and our "slumberverse") with increased self-awareness, purpose, and fulfillment. For within the enigma of dreams and the power of aspirations, we uncover the essence of who we are and who we aspire to become.

CONVERTING DREAMS INTO REALITY:

• **Dream Big:** Identify Your Dreams: Define what success looks like for you. Reflect on what truly moves you, what you're passionate about, and what sparks your curiosity.

• **Aim High**: Don't limit yourself. Allow your dreams to be as big, as bold, and as ambitious as you'd like them to be.

• **Embrace Reality:** Assess your reality. Understand your current situation, your strengths, and your areas for growth. Self-awareness is key to planning your journey.

• **Understand Limitations**: Identify potential obstacles. Understand that limitations are often temporary and can be overcome with perseverance.

• **Set Goals:** Specific and Realistic Goals: Break down your dreams into smaller, achievable goals. Make sure these goals are SMART (Specific, Measurable, Achievable, Relevant, Time-bound). Short-term goals will serve as steppingstones toward your long-term goals.

• **Develop Strategies**: Outline the steps you need to take to achieve your goals. This could involve further education, networking, or developing new skills.

• **Plan**: Understand the resources (time, money, skills) you have and those you'll need. Plan for how to acquire what you're missing.

• **Execute:** Start working on your plan. Remember, the journey of a thousand miles begins with a single step.

• **Persevere:** Expect setbacks. They are a part of every journey. Learn from your mistakes and keep going.

• **Monitor:** Track Your Progress: Keep a record of your accomplishments and challenges. This will help you understand what works and what doesn't.

• **Modify**: Be flexible. If something isn't working, change it. Your plan should be dynamic and adaptable.

• **Achieve:** Cross the Finish Line. Celebrate your successes, big and small. Each completed goal is a step closer to your dream.

• **Dream on**: Once you've achieved your dream, imagine new ones. Growth is a continuous journey of becoming a more resilient, adaptable, and fulfilled person.

Your Inner Light & Being

"Throughout our life we produce energy. We say things and do things, and every thought, every word, and every act carries our signature. What we produce as thoughts, as speech, as action, continues to influence the world, and that is our continuation body. Our actions carry us into the future. We are like stars whose light energy continues to radiate across the cosmos millions of years after they become extinct."
—Thich Nhat Hanh

For weeks, I found myself mysteriously drawn to a local consignment store. At the back, a peculiar painting hung, imbued with an ethereal quality. It portrayed a woman with seven eyes: two located in their typical positions, two adorning her palms, two on her feet's soles, and one in the middle of her forehead. Draped in pearls and crowned, a resplendent halo glowed around her head. The woman, her skin pale as the moon, sat cross-legged, a fully bloomed lotus nestled in her left hand. A circle of monks and an array of symbols surrounded her, but the painting bore no artist's signature, the meaning of its intricate details a complete mystery to me. This artwork played on my heart as no other had done before.

Three months later, when the owner of the store was going out of business, the painting—now known to me as a Thangka, a depiction of the Buddhist deity "White Tara"—took up a massive space on my wall. It was an eighteenth- or nineteenth-century ceremonial piece, crafted in the Nag Tang style, painted by some unknown Buddhist monk, I learned, as a form of meditation. Monks do not sign their works, as it is considered a sign of hubris—unlike fledgling authors. The painstaking effort put into the creation of a Thangka could span months, if not longer. Over time, the painting filled me with a sense of positive energy, and my life began to undergo a surreal transformation.

Here's what happened: I was scheduled for a thyroid biopsy and experienced a spontaneous remission of the tumor. I penned a bestselling novel, *Red Bird*, became a novice guest writer at the University of Oxford's International Summer School at Exeter College in the UK, visited the mystical Stonehenge, embraced yoga, launched a company, lectured in Moscow, graduated as the co-valedictorian of my master's program at The George Washington University, and witnessed my children flourish. But my exploration into the *mystical* didn't end there. One evening, after watching a documentary about a woman from Michigan who photographed strange light energies, I decided on a whim to take photos around my house at night.

To my surprise and horror, one image around the White Tara captured a spectral monk, clad in orange robes, looking directly into the camera! His gaze, warm yet piercing, jolted me into a terrified frenzy, where I screamed so loudly and trembled so much when I fled to the bedroom, I woke my worried (and disgruntled) husband.

Whether the Thangka was truly magical or a placebo, it didn't matter to me—what mattered is that having the privilege of being the keeper of a White Tara awakened my curiosity and inner light.

In the following days, while perusing a local bookstore, a *National Geographic* cover caught my eye: a portrait of an exiled Buddhist monk named Thich Nhat Hanh, radiating warmth and humility even through the glossy print. I devoured the feature about his teachings and philosophies, deeply resonating with his call for mindful living and compassionate service to others. His wisdom and words bored through and into the chambers of my soul. Later, as I delved into his books, I discovered a chapter in one of them named after my husband and me!

This synchronicity opened the door to new realms of possibilities I hadn't before considered. Call it a placebo effect or a coincidence or discredit it as the stuff of nonsense—but I consider it supernatural intervention. If a person can *think* themselves sick and create an ulcer in their stomach, shouldn't a human also possess an ability to *believe* him or herself healthy and capable of boundless Love, and all the greatness they and this universe have to offer?

Embracing these uncanny occurrences, I invited the spectral monk—whom I named Ito, Tibetan for "light"—into our home to freely visit.

Despite these beautiful external events and inner transformations, life still had its trials. Tribulations and setbacks are a natural part of the human experience and impossible to avoid. As sentient beings on this planet, we are bound to suffering and imperfection just as we are free to love and enlighten. The key, I feel, is to minimize the former as much as possible within ourselves, and accept our imperfection, as a form of internal ikebana. Ikebana is an Eastern form of flower arranging. It focuses on simplicity, minimalism, and the appreciation of negative space.

The arrangements often incorporate a sense of *asymmetry* and emphasize nature's *imperfect* beauty in existing materials. But ikebana is not just about arranging flowers; it is regarded as meditative and a contemplative practice. Practitioners aim to capture the essence and spirit of nature through their arrangements and express their individual interpretation of the natural world. The practice requires a deep understanding of various principles, such as line, shape, space, and color, as well as an appreciation for the seasons.

And boy, do I have a newfound appreciation for seasons, particularly those of the hurricane variety. In 2022, we lost our home and possessions to Hurricane Ian. We fled with our cats and the clothes on our backs as flood waters rose and rushed through our tiny living space. In an instant, almost everything we owned was gone! Imagine not having underwear or even a toothbrush. Suddenly, we didn't own a bed, a pillow, a piece of furniture, pots, pans, jewelry, computers, printers, appliances, lamps, or electronics. All our mementos, including my great grandmother's bible and our children's baby pictures? Gone. Food? Nope. Water? No. We found ourselves suddenly homeless—but I remembered: I'd been here before. And I survived.

Astonishingly, I wasn't heartbroken but felt liberated and lighter. We were in shock, yes. But others around us had it much worse—they'd lost pets or loved ones who'd drowned. Our *stuff* was of little consequence compared to our neighbor's anguish. When they could, friends and family showed up to help us clear debris. They offered love in the form of squeegees, temporary living spaces, and hugs. Amidst the wreckage, we discovered the White Tara unscathed, a beacon of light in the storm's aftermath. This disaster cemented friendships and we grew closer to loved ones and friends. It elevated my sense of gratitude, and it enhanced our compassion. We rolled up our sleeves, considered new adventures and possibilities—and just —let go.

In the vast and wondrous panorama of existence, I truly feel that each human being, like the White Tara, is a beacon of light, an embodiment of the infinite, divine universe, especially during a storm. This light glows within each one of us, and it is our intrinsic power, our potential, our Truth. In other words, we are angels without wings, made manifest, when we choose to turn on those switches of light. I view human beings as inexhaustible reservoirs of strength, compassion, creativity, and wisdom, attributes that define us as uniquely human, each a universe unto ourselves but part of the whole cosmos—if we choose to unburden ourselves of the sometimes-scary or stiff masks we wear—the masks designed to hide our pain or keep others away or assist in our rigid conformity.

There will always be moments when life's tempests dim your light, when your vision is clouded by adversity, fear, abuse, torture, destruction, disasters, or despair. Yet during such moments, your inner light, your energy, cannot be extinguished —only transformed. Energy, according to the fundamental concept of physics, can never be destroyed—and you, dear human, are energy. And since time is an illusion, a human construct, our light is an enduring flame, kindled by the primal fires of the cosmos, and sustained by the fundamental energy of existence extended to us through Source.

Alternatively, there exists another undeniable reality: Many of us grapple with various hardships, depression, isolation, turmoil, breakdowns, and disappointments. Yet, our exterior selves often hide our inner turmoil. We've mastered the art of concealing our struggles in a world that favors a faux and virtual "look at me doing better than you" attitude. We're adept at responding with an unassuming "Fine," when asked how we are. We're experts with our own convincing façade of normalcy.

Expressing our inner truths feels overwhelming when it looks and feels as if everyone else leads a perfect life. Additionally, there's always the lingering fear of negative reactions or worse, rejection. Occasionally, we simply can't bear to confront our actual circumstances, so we bury them in work, debt, spa treatments, shopping, sports, thrill-seeking, or with substance abuse—anything to avoid our pain.

If we were aware of the authentic narratives that lie beneath the surface of every human, we'd probably engage each other with heightened kindness and understanding. We might recognize that fear sometimes masks itself as anger, that sorrow takes the shape of aloofness, or that emotional pain often disguises itself as cynicism, anger, or humor. Remember, reactions usually conceal raw realities hidden inside hurting souls.

Being mindful of our words, our philosophies, our sweeping assumptions, and thoughtless judgments, and recognizing that amongst us walk individuals who bear silent wounds, opens worlds for us. Occasionally, those who hurt the most might be standing right beside us, feigning smiles, or agreement, while we unknowingly add to their pain. Or it could be us, the wounded ones, fighting back tears and striving to fade away from a crowd that at first appears as if they have it all together.

Life is fraught with challenges and every one of us faces silent struggles. It's an unspoken act of kindness to assume that many people among us are far more fragile than they appear. This is where extending a measure of grace is not only appropriate but honorable. After all, the greatest tragedy isn't extending unneeded empathy; it's the possibility of someone desperately needing it and us overlooking, making fun of, or ignoring that need.

The dance of your inner light, much like photons under gentle observance, shapes the rhythm of your life. Your inner light is like a laser in the grand choir among a cosmic orchestra. Your light is your essence, your heartbeat, and your signature tune. Allow your light to shine and sing (or hum if you consider yourself an introvert like me), not just for yourself, but also for others, illuminating paths, offering hope, and inspiring journeys or change.

To connect with your inner spark is to embark on the greatest adventure of your life! It is to journey inward, to explore the depths of your being, to discover and harness your latent potential and bring forth your talents! It is also to journey outward. Discover, explore, enrich, and learn. Be curious. This inner and outer exploration is both a challenge and a reward, a journey that unfolds with the patient unveiling of each moment, each choice, each act.

Post-hurricane, my daughter and I embarked on a cross-country road trip from Southern Florida to Las Vegas, something I likely wouldn't have done if we hadn't lost our home—because I initially viewed it as tiring and expensive. By the end of our trip, as we hiked a moderately difficult trail at Red Rock Canyon with our dear friend Debra, I realized I no longer had a little girl, but got to know the heart and light of an intelligent, vibrant, new best friend—a "grown ass" woman who happens to call me "mama." I saw my daughter in a different light—capable, strong, confident, and filled to the brim with love.

I spontaneously decided to make a detour into Albuquerque during my lone journey back home. As I found myself wandering through the charming streets of Old Town, I couldn't resist exploring local shops. Among them, one store caught my attention, showcasing the exquisite craftsmanship of Navajo jewelers and artists. Engaging in conversation with the store's owner, who happened to be a Navajo himself, I was pleasantly surprised when his "professor" joined our discussion.

The professor and I soon found ourselves engrossed in a captivating conversation about Brazilian Jujitsu. While I had only dabbled in the discipline for a brief period, my passion for it remained strong. I confessed that I longed for a discipline I'd left behind. Our dialogue gradually shifted toward deeper topics, such as honor and love. Intrigued by the professor's vast knowledge, I decided to test his familiarity with the works of

Rumi. To my delight, he responded with a knowing nod and a hearty laugh, revealing that he was indeed well-acquainted with Rumi's teachings. The professor pointed to the owner of the store and shared that this man shared the same name as the beloved poet himself: Rumi. I learned that day that Rumi means "rock" in Navajo—another synchronicity not to be ignored.

Know that your trail is not always a solitary one. Each one of us, a universe in our own right, connects with others through the radiant threads of our inner light, intertwining, and creating a magnificent show of human and Godly existence. Energy comingles—and "like" energy attracts like energy. As your inner light shines, it has the power to ignite the same in others, sparking a cascade of illumination that uplifts and transforms the world around us. You'll make new friends and cherish the old ones...but you'll also transition away from energies or friendships that drain your well-being and spirit. Sometimes this is hard at first, to let go of the familiar, but then this release eventually relieves and raises your resonance.

Your inner light, your quintessential self, the real you, *unmasked* and free from the chains of convention, criticism, and fear, is the lens through which you should perceive and interact with the world. It is an instrument of your clarity and service. It is through this lens that you recognize the same light in others, understanding the profound interconnection of all life, and embracing our shared humanity.

In the end, your inner light is more than a metaphor for potential. It is a testament to the power of your unique soul and spirit, a symbol of your capacity to overcome, to innovate, to empathize, to create, and to love. It is a reminder, as I once read somewhere, that we are more than physical beings on a corporeal journey; we are spiritual beings on a *human* journey, each of us a radiant spark of the cosmic whole. So, shine brightly, live boldly, and let your inner light guide you on the trip of a lifetime! And again, loosen your lotus!

. . .

Understanding the spiritual dimension of life

The spiritual dimension of a human's life refers to a person's quest for meaning, purpose, and connection beyond the physical and material realities of existence. It encompasses one's values, beliefs, and inner consciousness, and reflects how we relate to ourselves and to one another, to nature, and to the transcendent, whatever form that might take—whether it's God, the Universe, the Divine, or an elevated state of consciousness.

Spirituality can manifest in many ways, and it is highly individualistic, often shaped by personal experiences, cultural context, and philosophical or religious beliefs. It is not confined to religious practices, though for many, religion serves as a deeply powerful and personal conduit for spiritual exploration. But at its core, the spiritual dimension involves a profound sense of awareness having little to do with the dogmas of religion. It's about recognizing the inherent interconnectedness of all things, acknowledging the mystery and awe-inspiring aspects of being human, and seeking to transcend the boundaries of the self to experience a sense of love, unity, and wholeness with the universe, or Source—or God.

Continuing my path in Albuquerque, I was gifted by the universe with an extraordinary encounter. I crossed paths with a remarkable individual named Dean Johnson, also known by his spiritual name, "Little Lake." A native of Taos Pueblo, Little Lake is a living fusion of the mystical and material worlds.

Little Lake is the proprietor of a unique sanctuary named Smoke Signals; a gallery dedicated to peace pipes. These are not mere objects, but fragments of a sacred tradition handed down through the ages, a tradition of which I was woefully uninformed. Each pipe, he said, was a symphony of elements, meticulously handcrafted from cedar wood, harvested from the serene expanses of Taos Mountain. The sacred pipestone, a heart of some of his masterpieces, was a traveler itself, journeying from the soils of Minnesota. Each was adorned with delicate yet sturdy turquoise, bone, basalt, obsidian, or feathers, an artistic harmony of nature and spirit.

Despite his ethereal aura, Little Lake was firmly rooted in the tangible world as well. He once donned the suit of an executive at Intel, juggling the dynamics of the corporate world. Yet, his ancestors called to him, whispering through the smoke of the pipe, guiding him to his spiritual path and destiny as a forger of peace.

For a brief span of time, I was privileged to join Little Lake on his spiritual path. The teachings, the insights, and the wisdom I gleaned during our short journey were transformative. As we reached the culmination of our discussion, he gifted me one of his peace pipes. With a smile, he told me that I was not the pipe's owner, but its keeper. As he entrusted me with the pipe, he wrote down his prayer for me, "May the Spirits of the Taos Pueblo bring you harmony and countless blessings." The echo of his words followed me long after our paths diverged, inspiring me in ways I never anticipated.

The spiritual dimension often drives one's search for life's deeper meaning, prompting questions such as: Why are we here? What is the purpose of life? What does it mean to live a good life? How do I connect with something larger than myself? These profound inquiries often lead one to positive change and a profound sense of fulfillment, even if we don't always find the answers.

Furthermore, the spiritual dimension is crucial for overall well-being. It provides a source of hope, resilience, and strength in times of crisis. It nurtures compassion, empathy, and altruism, fostering a sense of responsibility toward the well-being of others and the planet. In essence, the spiritual dimension of a human's life invites us to delve deeper into our external existence, encourages us to live authentically, and enhances our capacity to appreciate the magnificent power and beauty found in a seed or reflect on the profound mysteries of the cosmos. It's a journey of micro to macro transcendence, and it shapes our lives in profoundly meaningful ways.

The role of Sacred Spirit in resilience and perseverance

The "sacred spirit" or "spiritual dimension" of a person's life plays a significant role in cultivating perseverance and resilience too. These qualities are often developed in the crucible of life's trials, and it's in these moments that the spiritual dimension often shines its brightest light, offering hope, strength, and wisdom.

At its core, our sacred spirit is our wellspring of inner strength. It is the invincible aspect of our "light being" that is not defined by external circumstances, but rather draws from the depths of something greater and beyond humanity. This interconnectedness is felt when we tap into the great universal reservoir, which enables us to navigate life's storms with grace, wisdom, and unwavering resilience.

Likewise, perseverance, the capacity to remain steadfast in the face of adversity, also bolsters our spiritual dimension. Our sacred spirit transcends immediate challenges. It considers a greater vision. It inspires us to stand firm, not to resist defeat, but because we are anchored in a purpose. Our spirit is larger than us, and it calls us to rise higher than our difficulties. We should get to know this inner guide just as we get to know and love a great friend.

In many spiritual traditions, hardships are not considered unfortunate events to be endured, but as provocateurs for character development. This perspective helps us to see beyond our fleeting bouts of pain and discomfort and to imagine the potential we have for healing and transformation.

SYNCHRONICITIES

Synchronicities, or meaningful coincidences, are sparks of enlightenment that appear related but are not causally connected. The concept was introduced by psychiatrist Carl Jung, who believed these occurrences have deep psychological and spiritual implications. However put to words, synchronicities are ancient and subtle messages of the universe.

Synchronicities offer us a sense of interconnectedness and unity. They highlight the idea that all things and events are somehow connected and promote a holistic worldview. When unexpected connections reveal themselves, they inspire a sense of awe, wonder, and curiosity about our world and give light to our hope. Synchronicities encourage us to remain open to life's mysteries and pleasant surprises. Such openness enhances creativity and playfulness.

Sometimes, synchronicities are perceived as affirmations or validations from the universe. For example, if you've been pondering a significant decision, a synchronistic event might be interpreted as a "sign" that you're on the right path. Alternatively, during times of stress, grief, or uncertainty, synchronicities may provide comfort and reassurance, especially if they help you make sense of a difficult situation or you find meaning within them. My synchronicities have arrived in the form of cardinals, human angels, timely aid, support, windfalls, and spontaneous healing or in music.

From a spiritual perspective, synchronicities often deepen one's faith or belief in a higher power, or open windows to the underlying order of the universe with lightning glimpses into the mysterious, the divine, or the transcendent. This in turn, may provide a richer, more profound sense of life's possibilities.

God & Faith—A Personal Journey

"I believe in Spinoza's God, who reveals himself in the lawful harmony of all that exists, but not in a God who concerns himself with the fate and the doings of mankind."
—Albert Einstein

My grandfather was a steadfast atheist. He was adamant in his disbelief, rejecting the traditional image of a deity atop a cloud, one flanked by angelic harp players behind pearly gates, meting out snobbish inclusivity or eternal damnation. Albert J. Wise declined to accept even Spinoza's pantheistic God, feeling it a betrayal of his background in engineering.

Indeed, Albert, my grandfather, was a resolute German man, grounded with a down-to-earth sense of humor, an appreciation for a well-aged scotch, and a curiosity for the natural phenomenon of energy. As an electrical engineer, ham radio operator, and private subcontractor for a couple of US-based nuclear facilities, he prided himself on his scientific acumen, diligent work ethic, and logical approach. And he deemed religion a ruse for the masses, crafted to manipulate base human impulses or incite conflicts in the name of divinity.

As a misanthrope, he carried a palpable disdain for most people and was often prone to outbursts of anger. For a period, I was under his guardianship before being remanded by social workers into foster care. They deemed a one-legged, atheistic electrical enthusiast an unsuitable caretaker for a child, particularly a young girl. They claimed that my becoming a ward of the court was a preferable alternative. And his influence, they asserted, was detrimental. Ours was a tearful parting. Authorities painted my grandfather as an ill-tempered, abusive man, but my memories of him are colored by nothing but love. He fostered in me a love for reading, a fascination for astronomy, and a passion for understanding the workings of the universe. He even introduced me to Nikola Tesla's groundbreaking patents! My grandfather was unlike anyone else I knew.

One wintery day, he sent me off to school—St. Paul's Catholic School—dressed in trousers. Having heavily snowed the previous night, my five-year-old self struggled through the knee-deep flakes to reach class, only to be immediately dismissed for wearing slacks.

In those days, girls donning pants at a private religious school was deemed "sinful" because one might glimpse the outline of my vagina and be irreparably damaged or unable to control impure "urges." I was too young to comprehend my "transgression." All I knew was the tears streaming down my face as I retraced my steps to my grandfather's workshop. His reaction was explosive, and that was it—I never returned to that Catholic school, much to my devout grandmother's dismay and mortification.

My grandfather scoffed at the notion that a dress code was crucial to maintaining a girl's modesty. He grumbled about the purported equality of creation, and how it was nonsensical to expect women to bear the burden of men's morality, especially if men deemed themselves superior to women. In his view, the patriarchal world and religion had little, if anything, to do with divinity or love.

We embarked on what I fondly refer to as

my "Home Schooling Experiment."

Each morning, he'd teach me the differences among a multitude of colored electrical wires. He'd pour some scotch from a dusty bottle he kept hidden behind a ham radio. We'd sit at one of his large work benches with books about gravity, mathematics, nuclear power, or electricity and he'd ask me if I was ready to change the world. He never considered the fact I was five—or a *girl*. His mind was clear that children were sponges, capable of storing reams of data if other adults refrained from labeling them too young or incapable.

Our lessons often began with his thoughts about people or life, and then we moved on to physics versus engineering (engineers always won). We typically ended with a reading from the works of Mark Twain or Nikola Tesla, Max Planck, Albert Einstein, or Madam Curie. He'd smoke his cigar, his eyes glinting with delight as he explained electromagnetic fields or fusion, and I'd listen in awe, absorbing as much as my young mind could handle.

My grandfather taught me to solder circuit boards, assemble radios, and wire electrical systems. There was a constant smell of solder and hot plastic in the air, mixed with the aroma of his scotch and cigars. Looking back, mixing smoke and alcohol with electricity was likely a severe OSHA violation. Yet to this day, whenever I catch a whiff of a cherry-scented cigar, I'm instantly transported to his workshop, surrounded by the chaos of old appliances, radios, spools of copper, a fascinating aluminum-type material that if coiled, remarkably righted itself, glass capacitors, wire, circuit boards, tuning forks, and my grandfather's unending enthusiasm for discovery. Occasionally, men in suits showed up and he'd shoo me out the door and tell me to go spend time with grandma.

In the evenings, we'd sometimes take short strolls down the

railroad tracks. He'd lean on his cane, his one-legged silhouette outlined against a setting sun, and I'd skip along beside him, trying to match his impressive pace. He'd point out constellations and planets in the sky, teaching me their names and the myths behind them. But our religious studies were nonexistent, except when he'd encourage me to question everything. His Truth, he said, was science.

Our neighbors and other authority figures thought this unconventional schooling bizarre. My grandmother lamented about how I was missing out on normal childhood experiences like learning hymns, reciting prayers, attending Sunday school, and wearing dresses. But looking back, I wouldn't trade my grandfather's experiments for all the dresses in the world.

As I grew, my grandfather's lessons remained. I found myself seeing the world through his lens of science, curiosity, and skepticism. When I attended university and aced my classes as a valedictorian, I had my grandfather to thank.

He passed away when I was nineteen. I'd just taken a job as a freelance sports and feature correspondent for a local newspaper. I covered football games and investigative pieces. He was so proud. By then, he'd retired and spent his days running a small airport in rural Ohio and flying his own Cessna. Once I cleared my hurdles of grief, I was left with the legacy of his unconventional wisdom and a love for learning.

Before he died, he presented me with a challenge coin regarding, what he claimed, was a time travel experiment. I'm still not permitted to disclose the details—until I'm eighty! I have his cobbled book and notes on Nikola Tesla patents and a message from him that reads, "Energy is the real God." And for an atheist, he unwittingly turned out to be the best influence for the existence of God I ever had, through his largely unwitnessed capacity for love.

. . .

Often, the perception of the Christian God is misconstrued as a fearsome, "fire and brimstone" entity, a deity who is intolerant of any perspectives that deviate from His own.

As a ward of the state and a foster child, my initial understanding of God was shrouded in trepidation. Any inquiries about the Bible or God deemed challenging or inconvenient by adults outside of my grandfather, were met with stern warnings of divine punishment or I was accused of being under the devil's influence and ripe for exorcism.

The idea of an omniscient, omnipotent God so interested in my thoughts that he'd punish me for asking questions (or cast me into the foster care system), seemed inexplicable, even to my young mind. Moreover, if my actions contradicted the beliefs of one of our rural and conservative community members, I was met with scorn or judgment, an irony given the divine edict I was taught, which instructed me to love one's neighbor and refrain from passing judgment.

Furthermore, my early readings of the Holy Bible suggested that women were mere accessories in the grand scheme of all things divine, relegated to the roles of slaves, concubines, wives, and servants. A female's credibility seemed subservient, our worthiness of love dependent on our sacrifice at the altar of matrimony and our identities and power solely dependent on how well we married. Such impressions drove me toward a state of agnosticism, even, for a while, atheism.

However, the passing of years gifted me with a profound realization. God, as I came to understand, is not vindictive or malicious. People can be. Instead, God represents energy, ascension, and most importantly, *Love*. This divine presence is not confined within the physical walls of churches, but pulsates within the hearts of people, resonates in the bloom of a flower, or mirrors itself in the innocent eyes of a child or an animal. We tend to lean toward hate and scorn in those moments when we are ignorant, feel threatened, are resentful, confused, or jealous.

The portrayal of a ruthless and war-hungry God that was

fed to me in my impressionable years appeared to be more of a tool for societal control, the promotion of nationalism, or used as a pacifier for those toiling in mundane jobs or prison. I viewed God as an imaginary and rigid deterrent from independence, self-exploration, curiosity, accountability, or pursuing passions in the short span of life before death's calling. How wrong was I! The concept of sin was, instead, my main problem.

Sin typically refers to an offense or transgression against God's divine law, as established by a particular religious system. It is associated with wrongdoing, disobedience, or actions considered morally or ethically unacceptable. Different religions have varying interpretations and teachings of sin, as well as different beliefs about its consequences, and how it should be addressed. In many religious traditions, sin is viewed as creating separation and distance between individuals and their respective deities.

In Christianity, for example, sin is viewed as a violation of God's commandments and a condition inherited by humanity due to the original sin of Adam and Eve—they ate an apple from a forbidden tree after Eve was allegedly tempted by a snake. This first couple's ensuing punishment from God still seems harsh to me. He cast them out of paradise and into the wilds of hell on Earth.

From what I remember of my former Sunday school lessons, God didn't want humans to receive the knowledge of good and evil from an apple tree. Why? We, as parents, teach this same knowledge to our children in the hope they'll grow up to be productive, kind, and contributing members of society and refrain from violent tendencies. Nevertheless, Christians believe that sin disrupts the harmonious relationship between humans and God, resulting in a need for repentance, forgiveness, and reconciliation with God through faith in Jesus Christ, who came to Earth and took the form of a man, and died on a cross for our sins.

In Islam, sin is considered a violation of Allah's commands as revealed in the Qur'an. Muslims believe that engaging in "sinful acts" creates spiritual impurity and leads to negative consequences in this life and in the afterlife. Repentance, seeking forgiveness, and striving to follow Allah's guidance are seen as ways to address and overcome sin, more similar to Christianity than most adherents, whether they be Muslim or Christian, care to admit.

It's important to note that the concept of sin varies significantly among religions, and even within different denominations, or sects of the same religion. The understanding and interpretation of sin often depend on specific religious teachings, scriptural interpretations, the cultural contexts involved, and often too, the utter failings of humanness rooted in spiritual arrogance.

In a broad sense, sin is considered a breach of religious laws or ethical norms. While it serves to establish moral guidelines and acceptable community standards, the concept of sin presents humans with a few hindrances:

- **Guilt and Shame:** One of the biggest problems with the concept of sin is the guilt and shame it induces in individuals. If someone is constantly berated or worried about sinning, how does this lead them to a divine spiritual relationship with God? It doesn't. It leads people instead, to fear, resentment, excessive guilt, stress, anxiety, and lowered self-esteem. This is especially true if the person feels that they can't live up to extraordinarily high moral standards set by their religious leaders, under tests impossible to pass.

- **Intolerance and Judgment:** The concept of sin can be used to justify discrimination and prejudice against those who are perceived to have sinned, leading to social divisions, protest, violence, abuse, and war. It fosters an environment of distrust and intolerance, rather than building love, peace, empathy, or understanding. Physically punishing or killing another human being based on harsh judgment is *not* leadership or Godly. It is cowardly. The blood of another being remains on your hands and heart—and you become accountable for interfering with God's plan for this individual, over their path to divine forgiveness and transcendence.

Consequently, forcing someone to adopt a code of conduct, clothing, or behavior does not make one holy or powerful, but weak. If violence or bans are the only way to institute this sort of control, you've lost your potency and your people. There is a Muslim saying, "A man of God would never burn or harm a temple of any kind—regardless of religion." Man and woman are made in God's image. This makes each of us divine and equal temples that should be revered and protected, rather than defaced, demeaned, or destroyed.

- **Conflict with Modern Ethics and Laws:** Some religious sins do not align with contemporary societal norms. For instance, certain aspects of sexuality, gender identity, and freedom of expression may be deemed sinful in some religious contexts but are accepted or protected by modern societal values or laws. This conflict causes confusion and distress for individuals who are part of these communities and condemning them is the opposite of love and non-judgment.

- **Reliance on External Validation:** The concept of sin often involves pleasing or displeasing a higher power or religious authority and winning their approval over divine transcendence. How does forcing a person to acquiesce to another's idea of God please the Divine? Such external validation usually results in individuals becoming more concerned about avoiding undue punishment rather than developing an internal sense of morality and ethical behavior.

- **Potential for Manipulation:** In the hands of the wrong individuals or institutions, the concept of sin is manipulated to control people's behavior, sometimes leading to abuse of power and corruption.

- **Impediment to Personal Growth and Freedom:** The fear of sinning usually inhibits personal growth, exploration, and freedom. In this context, the concept of sin might limit personal and intellectual freedoms and discourage people from exploring diverse ideas and lifestyles that are deemed *sinful* by others.

All religious or ethical systems potentially suffer *sin* problems because humans are fallible. When such challenges arise within a spiritual community, they should be carefully and objectively considered using circumspection, love, and compassion—leading to liberating and life-affirming communion with God.

Let us reconsider, for a moment, the notion of sin within God's realm, however you choose to define Him (or Her, or it). Instead of condemning actions, pronouns, words, or behaviors of others as *sinful*, perhaps we should turn inward to our own moral compass as our guide. Let us permit others to follow the path that the divine love within *their* hearts urges them to take —even if you don't agree. And is it more important to disagree? Or is it more important to be accepting and to *Love*? After all, the essence of divinity is not punishment, judgment, or control, but an expression of boundless ***Love***. And if we are all created in the image of God, wouldn't this, regardless of our gender, sex, or ethnicity, render us equals?

ATHEISM

Atheism is the absence or rejection of belief in the existence of any deities or gods. It is the position that asserts that there is no compelling evidence or convincing reason to believe in the existence of a higher power or divine beings.

Atheists typically hold a worldview that is based on naturalism, rationalism, and skepticism. They approach questions of existence, morality, and meaning from a secular and non-religious perspective. Atheism does not necessarily imply a denial of the possibility of a god or gods, but rather a lack of belief in the existence of God due to insufficient evidence.

It's important to note that atheism is not a unified belief system or philosophy. Atheists hold diverse views on various aspects of life, ethics, and the universe. Some may be actively opposed to religious beliefs and practices, while others may simply lack belief without actively rejecting the possibility. Atheism is a broad term, like Christianity, which encompasses a wide range of perspectives and attitudes toward religion and the existence of deities.

While it's important to note that individual beliefs and values vary greatly within any group, including among Christians and atheists, there are several aspects commonly associated with atheism that might offer beneficial perspectives to Christians.

These include:

- **Critical Thinking and Skepticism**: Atheists often approach religious claims with skepticism, encouraging critical examination of beliefs and values. This does not necessarily mean that atheists question the existence of God. This might inspire Christians to thoughtfully interrogate their own beliefs, strengthening their faith or leading to deeper understandings of the Divine.

• **Secular Ethics**: Atheists generally base their ethical systems on secular values, such as the well-being of conscious creatures or the idea of logic, the exercise of civility, common sense, fairness, or equality. Atheists often argue that one doesn't need to be religious to understand the difference between right and wrong or to embrace spirituality. Christians might learn from this by considering how they might examine some of their religious positions on secular grounds, contributing to broader societal conversations about morality and ethics, and in turn, strengthening their faith.

• **Religious Tolerance and Pluralism**: Since atheists don't adhere to a specific religious worldview, they are often more open to a variety of religious beliefs and traditions. This perspective might encourage Christians to be more accepting of religious diversity, fostering greater respect, and understanding among different faith communities. One thing I've always found refreshing is how kind and loving Buddhists are about the idea of Jesus Christ. Thich Nhat Hanh often uses examples found in Christianity to highlight points about the human condition and Buddhism. Additionally, most Christians and Muslims do not realize that the prophet Muhammad permitted Christians to pray in his mosque and that some mosques have Christian quotes carved upon their walls.

• **Science Appreciation**: Atheists often place a strong

emphasis on scientific understanding, adopting a worldview primarily informed by empirical evidence and reason. Christianity and science are not at odds, especially if a higher intelligence created both. They are, instead, flip sides of the same coin. Christians might learn from atheists' emphasis on science as a tool for comprehending the natural world and themselves.

• **Present-Moment Orientation**: Atheism often fosters a focus on the present, the *NOW* because it doesn't include beliefs about an afterlife. While Christians generally believe in life after death, they might also find value in concentrating on the present, enhancing their appreciation and connection to nature and reliance on this world for breath and sentient life, and their relationships with others.

• **Freedom of Thought**: Atheists often prioritize personal freedom when it comes to beliefs and opinions, appreciating diversity in thought. This might serve as a reminder for Christians to respect individuality within their community or foster a respectful environment where questions and differing interpretations are appreciated and welcomed.

Again, these are not definitive or universal attributes of all atheists, nor do I suggest that these traits are absent among Christians or Muslims or any other religious adherents. Rather, they represent some areas where interaction between seemingly polarized groups might lead to beneficial learning and greater peace. Mutual understanding and respectful dialogue among diverse beliefs often lead to enriched perspectives and greater diplomacy.

. . .

The Power of Prayer

What is prayer? Many of us regard prayer as a religious activity—a conscious appeal to a higher power. But beyond the confines of theology, prayer holds a deeper, profound metaphysical essence. A metaphysical understanding of prayer illuminates how it transcends religious dogmas to become a universal spiritual exercise, encapsulating humanity's longing for connection, wisdom, and transcendence.

Metaphysics, in the simplest terms, seeks to explain the fundamental nature of reality, including the relationship between mind and matter, substance and attribute, potentiality and actuality. It delves into aspects of existence that transcend physical phenomena—the "super" natural—not to be confused with ghosts or goblins or little green men—but simply viewed as aspects of phenomena, such as physics, consciousness, or nature we don't yet understand. Likewise, prayer transcends the physical—crossing boundaries of human perception to touch the metaphysical, divine, or otherworldly realms.

From a metaphysical perspective, prayer isn't merely an act of voicing our requests or complaints to a divine entity. It is a conduit to higher consciousness—a manifestation of our innate desire to connect with the universe's profound mystery and realize our unity with it. When we pray, we aren't just speaking to an external God; we are conversing with our innermost selves, made in the image of God, and reaching into a vast pool of cosmic consciousness, of which we are a part, to connect with the sacred.

The power of prayer lies in its ability to transform our consciousness. This transformation extends beyond mere emotional solace; it elevates our perception of existence. It allows us to perceive and interact with our reality on a more profound, spiritual level—and harness sacred power. Prayer, in its deepest sense, helps us tap into the divine and intelligent vibrational energy that permeates the universe and created every one of us. The words and feelings invoked during prayer create energetic waves that resonate with the universe's fundamental frequencies, cultivating a harmony between us and the cosmos, and its Source, however defined.

The Law of Attraction, a metaphysical theory, postulates that "like attracts like." Thus, the energetic resonance created during prayer attracts elevated experiences and circumstances that align with our projected energy. In other words, our prayers—laden with desires, hopes, and emotions—shape our reality—which leads to profound insight, prophecy, healing, creativity, prosperity, peace, joy, and Love.

Prayer, Chants and Mantras as a Pathway to Wisdom and Transcendence

Prayer, chants, and mantras are mediums of transcendence. They allow us to rise above our mundane concerns and first world problems, to connect with the timeless, eternal Divine, and to 'just be' in the *Now*. Through these mediums we experience moments when time pauses, and we find ourselves in the presence of the supernatural, where the finite self merges with the infinite consciousness, and offers us a gifted glimpse into the unity of all existence, and an opportunity for communion with supreme beings, bridging the chasm between the physical and spiritual.

Regardless of our religious beliefs or spiritual inclinations, embracing an understanding of prayer, chants, and mantras, and tapping into their powerful energies provides pathways to higher consciousness. Consider it a meditation of potential, an opportunity to interact with the universe's fundamental frequencies, and a platform for offering praise, gratitude, and connection to something beyond human.

God: A Tapestry of Perspectives

Throughout human history, the concept of a Supreme

Being, an all-knowing, all-powerful entity often termed "God," has been a topic of deep introspection, heated debates, gruesome wars, and quiet contemplation. Different cultures, societies, and individuals, from the mystics of the East to the philosophers of the West, have striven to understand and articulate their unique perspectives of God. These myriad interpretations reflect the diversity of human experience, the boundless realms of our collective imagination, and the shared quest for understanding the purpose and meaning of existence.

A common view of the Christian God is that of a "fire and brimstone" creator, a jealous God who has no room or tolerance for outside perspectives (or other gods) and one that will damn humans to an eternity in Hell if they fail to strictly adhere to His commandments or dare blaspheme the Holy Spirit. This was the God I was taught.

I prefer the idea of a benevolent Creator, an entity that crafted the universe and everything within it. This perspective resonates across many religious and spiritual traditions, attributing the marvels and mysteries of existence to a divine Architect. God, in this understanding, is an ever-present guardian, a reservoir of infinite love, compassion, and wisdom, guiding humanity toward moral righteousness and spiritual awakening.

Yet, there is another perspective, perhaps closer to my ideology, one that portrays God as an Impersonal Force, a cosmic energy that pervades all existence. This viewpoint is prevalent in certain strands of Hinduism, Buddhism, and Taoism. It's also echoed in some contemporary spiritual philosophies and contends that God is not some vague external entity hiding in the clouds with lightning bolts, ready to mete out punishment. God is the underlying *reality* of all things, omniscient and omnipotent, everywhere, within, above, and all around us. Here, understanding and experiencing God is akin to awakening to our interconnectedness and realizing the sanctity of ***all*** life.

Another perspective, stemming from the agnostic or atheistic worldview, challenges the existence of a traditional God the way my grandfather did. In this light, God may be seen not as a literal entity but as a symbolic representation of humanity's highest ideals, aspirations, and ethical standards. God embodies virtues like love, kindness, knowledge, science, forgiveness, justice, and courage, serving as a moral compass that guides human behavior.

Alternatively, some perceive God as the Universe itself, or Pantheism, as Spinoza and Einstein notably did. In this view, God does not exist apart from the universe but is entirely synonymous with it and its laws. Every star, planet, life form, atom, and quantum particle is part of God, making every scientific discovery a revelation of the celestial.

From the viewpoint of Process Theology, God is not omnipotent in the traditional sense, but evolves *with* the universe, affected by the actions and experiences of sentient beings. This perspective views God as a companion in our cosmic journey, sharing in our joys, sorrows, hopes, and dreams —and without us, there is no *Him*.

What these perspectives underline is not so much the disparities but an astonishing diversity in human understanding —and their commonalities. Each viewpoint brings with it a unique lens to perceive the divine, allowing for a more comprehensive and nuanced understanding of what God might signify —but—in the end, whatever your beliefs, or another's, it's ***all***, on some level, about the same God.

At its core, discourse about God is a mirror to our collective and individual human consciousness, reflecting our evolving understanding of the universe, existence, and ourselves. It embodies humanity's inherent longing for love, understanding, community, connection, purpose, and the quest to transcend the oft suffering and transient nature of biological life. It may well be a point of agreement that leads us to similarly define or feel God, but one we call by different names.

For me, the quest to understand God is not about finding definitive answers or demanding concrete proof, or miracles on demand. It isn't about arguing *my* God over yours. That's religion—and religion typically requires an enemy to fight in order to thrive. God is not about sitting in the front pew of church every single Sunday or adhering to a conscripted set of manmade laws. Instead, God is about broadening our perspectives, opening our hearts to a multitude of interpretations, and acknowledging that each person's search for meaning may lead us down different paths. This quest for God *is* about embracing diversity, fostering tolerance, and meditating on and praying for peace. It is cultivating an open dialogue that enriches our collective wisdom, rather than reducing it to ash and hopelessness through war, anger, control, force, or violence. But most of all, God is about *LOVE*.

Whether we perceive God as a divine Creator, an impersonal cosmic energy, a symbol of virtues, the Universe itself, or a companion in evolution, each perspective brings us closer to understanding the vast, intricate, and beautiful spiritual veil behind our incredible existence. In exploring these varied perspectives, I strive to know God and to comprehend the deepest aspects of myself, and the profound mysteries of the cosmos we inhabit—and always harbor hope that we will someday become elevated humans deeply rooted in this awe-inspiring Love.

In the end, we may discover that the concept of God, in all its myriad forms, serves as a meaningful testament to humanity's ceaseless desire to explore, understand, and connect with mysteries that lie beyond the grasp of our immediate senses and consciousness horizons. And in this endeavor, we may also one day find ourselves surprisingly bound by a shared quest with beings from other planets or dimensions, all made by the same *God*—on a similar quest for love, meaning, understanding, and connection, one that may encapsulate a vast sentient experience.

THE ROLE OF FAITH

Faith, in its broadest sense, transcends the bounds of any religious belief. It's an inherent power that lifts us when the path before us becomes obscured. Its energy moves us when everything else seems to stand still. Faith is not an attribute owned solely by the devout or religious, but an innate human ability, a universal element woven into our shared humanity.

Faith, as well as I know it to be, is profound trust in the unseen, in the power of goodness, hope, and the resilience that lies within us and in the universe that surrounds us. It's believing, as a Christian, in a '*son rise*' when we're enveloped by darkness. It's trusting in the emergence of spring when surrounded by the harshness of winter. Faith is a testament to our human strength and optimism. It represents our instinctual yearning for peace and blessings within the depths of despair or conflict.

Faith is what inspires us to plant seeds under hardened soil and trust in their growth to yield fruit, even though we cannot *see* the process. It emboldens us to take that first step into the unknown with courage, even when we're frightened. Faith urges us to believe in the potential of our dreams, despite the hurdles. Faith offers us hope when we feel lost, like a sturdy staff to part a raging sea. In this way, faith goes beyond religiosity. It is inside, but not confined to churches, cathedrals, temples, or mosques. Faith exists in beating hearts, in the messages of the wind, in the magnificence of mountains, and along the flow of rivers. It is heard in the laughter of a child or the comforting silence between friends. It is found in the supportive embrace of a loved one. It is a sacred voice within us that says, "Despite everything, life is beautiful and worth fighting for."

Indeed, faith means trusting your journey, even when you can't see the destination. Sometimes, faith means surrendering control and acknowledging our smallness in the grand scheme of the universe. It is recognizing our capacity to traverse dimensions and elevate our souls. It's accepting that we don't always have all the answers. It is believing that questions themselves can lead to profound truths.

Hold on to your faith, not as some half-hearted religious obligation, but as a great manifestation of your human strength and spirituality. Let it guide you, inspire you, and uplift you. Above all, let it remind you that, no matter the hardships, you are capable of immense resilience, greater love, and extraordinary growth.

Remember too, faith is not just about believing in one thing or everything. It's about believing in yourself, in something greater than all of us, and the boundless potential planted in your soul. May faith always be your compass, illuminating your path, nurturing your dreams, and reminding you that you are a part of something much grander than the immediate confines of this illusory reality and fading body we think of as Life. You are a child of the cosmos, divine and supernatural—an angel of light made manifest!

Consciousness – A Gateway to Understanding

"You develop an instant global consciousness, a people orientation, an intense dissatisfaction with the state of the world, and a compulsion to do something about it. From out there on the moon, international politics looks so petty."
——Edgar Mitchell, Astronaut

Once the psychedelic psilocybin coursed its way through my veins, roughly thirty minutes post a significant intake, I found myself gently slipping away from the boundaries of reality, loosening the ties to my physical form. "I'm dying!" I thought, the veils of human perception systematically lifted from my mind like peeling an onion layer by layer. "I'm going to be sick!"

I heard a voice. "Let go..." it whispered. "Just...be." What remained of my essence, a radiant glow, began its spiral upward journey.

Invisible entities, akin to spectral apparitions, attempted to merge with my energy, hoping for a free ride. Yet, with each futile attempt, I would release their encroaching forms using deft maneuvers or dramatic nonhuman swirls. My luminescence mingled only with that which guided me higher into alternate dimensions, passing a variety of celestial beings and creatures along this journey. I wore a blindfold but could *see* my husband. He held up fingers I could count. I felt so much love for him and he glowed with a soft geometric grid of green light. I hugged him and we melded into a single unit of illumination. I had known him before and always—because time in this space had no existence. I had temporarily stepped outside the illusion and pierced the veil of the matrix.

I encountered Shamans, astral travelers from Earth, inhabiting the same metaphysical plane, their tattooed chests, and headdresses, and sticks through their noses, a ritual, they said, to enhance their journeys in a waking and walking dream. They instilled tranquility in my heart, reassuring me that I was not at the precipice of death, but upon the dawn of rebirth, an extraordinary opportunity to absorb divine wisdom. If I would surrender to the process, let go, and embrace the teachings, a more magnificent light of sacred knowing would unfurl before me.

Shortly afterward, I crossed paths with beings of pure light and a fascinating array of extraterrestrial life. Many remained indifferent, some shared empathetic smiles, while others engaged in a wordless exchange of thoughts. Eventually, everything transmuted into a timeless amalgamation of pure radiance and unbound love.

At the apex of my trip, I was greeted by Source, a sacred entity of undefined form, embodying a feminine intelligence of light I could somewhat understand. This entity commenced an upload of my consciousness, encoding within it whispered secrets of the cosmos. And then there was nothing—where I found everything.

THE MYSTERIES OF CONSCIOUSNESS: PERSONAL AND UNIVERSAL

Consciousness, both at a personal and universal level, has been a topic of deep contemplation and research for centuries. Even though we have made significant strides in understanding the workings of the human brain, the mysteries of consciousness remain largely unresolved. Here are a few of the questions surrounding consciousness:

- **Nature of Consciousness**: Is consciousness purely a product of the physical processes of the brain, or does it exist independently?

- **Hard Problem of Consciousness**: Coined by philosopher David Chalmers, this refers to the question: Why and how do physical processes in the brain give rise to the subjective, experiential aspect of consciousness?

- **Qualia**: This refers to our subjective experiences of the world, such as, what is red? Or what is the bitterness of coffee? And how do these qualitative experiences arise from the firing of neurons in the brain?

- **Consciousness and Reality**: How does consciousness relate to the external world? Is our perception of reality truly "real," or is it a construct of our consciousness?

- **Self-awareness**: How and why did consciousness evolve to include self-awareness? What is its function, and how does it relate to other cognitive processes?

- **Artificial Consciousness**: Can consciousness be

replicated in artificial systems? If so, what are the ethical implications of creating conscious machines?

- **Non-human Consciousness**: To what extent are animals or even plants conscious? How does this consciousness differ from human consciousness, if at all?

- **Altered States of Consciousness**: What happens to consciousness during altered states such as dreaming, under the influence of psychedelic substances, or in near-death experiences?

- **Unity of Consciousness**: How does the brain unify various sensory inputs into a single, coherent perception of the world?

- **Universal Consciousness**: Is there a shared, universal consciousness that all beings participate in? This question bridges science, philosophy, and spirituality.

In the last few years, new disciplines such as cognitive neuroscience, artificial intelligence, psychedelic treatments, and quantum physics have added more layers to the understanding (or misunderstanding) of consciousness. Yet, consciousness, for humans, remains one of the most challenging mysteries of the universe. It cannot be located or described or understood—it must be felt and experienced.

What is subconsciousness?

My husband is a certified clinical hypnotherapist, a profession that initially led me to conjure up unkind images from county fairs, carnivals, and the mortifying annals of the CIA's once clandestine MK-Ultra Program. I remembered sideshow spectacles wherein individuals surrendered their mental defenses to a somewhat disconcerting figure peddling the promise of mind control to an eager audience of voyeurs. Yet my understanding of hypnotherapy underwent a profound shift as my husband, David, shared insights from his training and practical sessions. When I felt comfortable, we practiced together.

David explained that hypnotherapy is not about the hypnotist controlling another's mind or actions, but about empowering individuals to seize control and reprogram their own mental constructs within the subconscious. The hypnotist, he claims, merely acts as a guide or technician for those ready to refurbish outdated or potentially self-harmful raw psyche data. This was a shift in perspective that left me surprised and hopeful. Could the subconscious mind really be manipulated in such a manner? Sure, he said. It is simply programming that needs to be rewired, discarded, or replaced.

David shared that the amygdala, an organ situated deep within our brains (along with the hypothalamus and caudate nucleus), is the seat of our emotions and subconscious mind. Commonly known as our primal brain, the amygdala harbors an array of raw feelings such as desire, greed, envy, lust, and hunger, as well as other attributes like extreme attachment. However, it's not just these powerful emotions that reside there.

According to David, the amygdala also harbors past traumas. It nurtures the vicious cycles of harmful habits and negative thinking that chain us to fear, insecurities, and destructive or addictive behaviors. This intricate programming persists within our brain, influencing our bodies and minds. Most of us remain completely ignorant and unaware of the extent of control it exerts over us. What's even more surprising is the realization that this programming can be altered and upgraded!

Several tools can aid us in reshaping or reprogramming our perceptions, including psychotherapy, music, art, meditation, prayer, physical exercise, and of course, hypnotherapy and kind words of encouragement. These paths may offer an appealing alternative to reset our minds and bodies, to release the burdens of the past, and to forgive ourselves and others. In doing so, they provide an avenue to heal not only from emotional distress but also physical ailments.

The idea in hypnotherapy is not to shut down the subconscious mind. The subconscious mind provides many benefits and is an essential component of the human experience through some of its key functions:

- **Information Storage**: The subconscious mind stores a vast amount of information that we don't need to consciously think about, like how to drive a car or use a smartphone. This includes everything from our learned behaviors to our beliefs, attitudes, and emotional responses.

- **Habit Formation**: The subconscious mind is instrumental in creating and maintaining habits. Repeated actions or thoughts can become automated processes in the subconscious, requiring little conscious effort to perform. This can be beneficial, such as when learning a new skill, but also challenging, if negative thinking patterns become ingrained.

- **Emotional Responses**: Our subconscious mind is responsible for our instantaneous emotional reactions to experiences. It's where our feelings are processed, and it influences our emotional responses to different situations based on past experiences and learned behavior.

- **Protective Mechanisms**: The subconscious mind helps protect us by alerting us to danger. It operates faster than our conscious mind and triggers an immediate physiological response (like the fight-or-flight response) when it perceives a threat.

- **Creativity and Problem-Solving**: While our conscious mind is logical and analytical, our subconscious mind is more imaginative and intuitive. It can make connections between disparate pieces of information, leading to creative insights and solutions. This is why you might have a sudden insight or "a-ha" moment when you're not consciously thinking about a problem.

- **Self-Preservation and Healing**: The subconscious mind governs our body's autonomous functions like heart rate, digestion, and cell regeneration, which are essential for our survival and healing.

Understanding and leveraging the power of the subconscious mind has significant impact on your life. Through techniques such as hypnotherapy, meditation, and cognitive behavioral therapy, *you* influence your subconscious mind to overcome negative patterns and promote healthier thoughts and behaviors. Think of it as remediation of the mind, where you're mitigating the damage of emotional malware and dysfunctional viruses.

Utilizing Consciousness to Enhance Your Quality of Life

Consciousness is the state of being aware of and able to think and perceive one's surroundings, thoughts, emotions, and experiences. Utilizing consciousness effectively enhances the quality of one's life.

Here are some ways to do this:

- **Mindfulness**: This is the practice of becoming more aware of the present moment, rather than dwelling in the past or anticipating the future. By training yourself to live in the now, you can reduce stress, improve your mental health, and derive more satisfaction from life.

• **Self-awareness**: Understand your thoughts, feelings, motivations, strengths, weaknesses, and behaviors. Self-awareness can help you navigate life with a clearer sense of purpose, make better decisions, and engage more effectively with others.

• **Emotional Intelligence**: This is the ability to understand, use, and manage your emotions in positive ways to relieve stress, communicate effectively, empathize with others, overcome challenges, and defuse conflict. High emotional intelligence can lead to healthier relationships and better career success.

• **Growth Mindset**: Consciousness allows us to realize that our abilities and intelligence can be developed. A growth mindset can enhance your ability to learn, grow, and face challenges.

• **Cognitive Restructuring**: This involves changing negative thought patterns into positive ones. It can help reduce anxiety and depression, improve stress management, and enhance your overall outlook on life.

• **Creativity and Innovation**: Consciousness allows us to dream, imagine, and create. Using it to fuel your creativity and innovation can lead to personal growth and fulfillment.

• **Meditation**: A practice that trains your mind to focus and redirect your thoughts. It can reduce stress, increase awareness of yourself and your surroundings, and increase your capacity for empathy and compassion.

- **Life-Long Learning**: With conscious effort, we can continue to learn and grow throughout our lives, increasing our understanding of the world and ourselves, and adding depth and richness to our experiences.

- **Healthy Lifestyle**: Conscious decisions about diet, exercise, sleep, and other lifestyle factors can have substantial effects on physical health and mental well-being.

- **Goal-Setting and Achievement**: Being conscious about setting and striving for goals can give a sense of purpose and direction, increasing satisfaction and happiness in life.

The application of consciousness or mindfulness or awareness (however you choose to define it) is more than a one-time task. It is a lifelong practice. And retooling your subconscious if it no longer serves your elevation is life changing.

Overcoming Fear & Its Shadows

"Fear can be good when you're walking past an alley at night or when you need to check the locks on your doors before you go to bed, but it's not good when you have a goal and you're fearful of obstacles. We often get trapped by our fears, but anyone who has had success has failed before."

—Queen Latifah

From my earliest recollections, my mother was a severe and uncontrollable storm of emotions that had the power to suddenly shift course and unleash her violent fury upon me without warning.

At the tender age of three, one autumn day turned into a terrifying scene with me huddled against a cold fridge, my mother brandishing a shotgun at my head.

I was no stranger to her violence, as it often took the form of hours of solitary confinement in a pitch-dark closet, or painful lashes from a belt. Yet, later in childhood, each bruise was hidden behind fabricated stories of tree-climbing adventures gone awry, or other well-rehearsed lies to soothe concerned adults in denial or deter outside intervention. I didn't want my mom to get into trouble. And she led me to believe I deserved her abuse because I was, as she said, an incorrigible child no one loved.

The courts and caseworkers, too, turned a blind eye to her mental illness, always pushing for familial reconciliation over acknowledging my chilling and dangerous reality. Everybody, except my grandfather, an uncle, and his wife, was in denial that my mother should not have had or been forced to raise children she did not want. My mother was diagnosed with paranoid schizophrenia post-divorce from a man I thought was my father, but even this stark revelation seemed to fall on deaf ears, lost in the bureaucracy of the "system." However, that particular autumn day, everyone involved was about to witness a miracle.

Mom demanded I stop being a baby and gaze upon her before she blew my head off, "so I can see the look on your face." My wrists covered my ears and my elbows touched as I slunk lower to the ground and deeper against the fridge, refusing to look.

My uncle, a Marine who just happened, thankfully, to be on leave, arrived at our home as tension peaked. He tried to coax the shotgun from my mother's hands. Duke, our Saint Bernard, ambled into the room. What happened next remains imprinted on my mind, a testament to an instinctive act of bravery. Ignoring my mother's screams and the blows struck to his head, Duke sat resolutely between us, staring down the barrel. His unyielding canine stance defused the situation, ultimately leading to my mother's transfer of the gun to my uncle, and her first trip to the Tiffin State Hospital for the Mentally Ill. This marked a temporary respite for me, but it wouldn't last long.

My mom was never criminally charged with anything. The entire event was dismissed as an unfortunate domestic situation because the truth was just too uncomfortable for adults to admit. Even as a child, I found this confusing. Surely, I thought, I must be unworthy of love if someone who tries to kill me isn't charged with attempted murder.

Two years later, on a serene spring morning, I was returned to my mother's home. She was healed, authorities claimed, her demons having been exorcised by a priest at our local parish. Nobody mentioned her electroconvulsive shock therapies, solitary confinements, or copious anti-hallucination meds.

I remember sheer curtains dancing in the breeze of the bedroom I shared with my two-year-old brother. The old Victorian home was owned by my grandparents, who hoped the added financial support might magically convert my mom into an award-winning parent. My brother, a toddler, bounced in his crib when my mother quietly entered our room. Her mascara-smeared face, haunted by an inscrutable madness, sent shivers spiraling down my spine.

"Isn't it a beautiful day?" she asked.

I gulped and nodded.

"In fact," she said with a mad laugh, "I think it's a beautiful day to die!" She pulled a butcher knife from behind her back. I was gripped with intense terror. The fear on my face made her laugh harder. We were cornered, my brother and me, destined to be innocent victims of an unfolding tragedy.

Yet again, the universe had other plans. The day that could have ended in disaster was transformed by an unexpected heroine. My grandmother, who had been gardening nearby, happened to peer through our bedroom window just in time. Her scream ripped through the morning tranquility, and her actions saved our lives. As she wrestled my mother, I escaped through the window, racing to my grandfather for help. Once more, my mother was committed, this time for a more extended period, and I never lived under her roof again.

These experiences taught me the harsh realities of life at a very young age, but they also instilled in me a spirit or resiliency. From the loyalty of a dog to the bravery of my grandmother and my uncle, I learned the true meaning of courage. They taught me that fear can be confronted, that even in the face of extreme danger, we have the capacity to overcome. It's through these trials that I learned to stand tall, to fight, and, above all, to do more than just survive—I learned to love.

Fear is a natural, powerful, and primitive emotion that involves a universal biochemical response as well as a highly individualized emotional response. It alerts us to the presence of danger or a threat of harm, be it physical or psychological. Fear is experienced by all humans and most animals. It's automatic and fundamental to our survival because it triggers the body's fight-or-flight response to preserve our physical "matter." However, when fear grows persistent or excessive, or hinders daily life, managing and overcoming it might feel debilitating and impossible. Yet it's essential.

As you might imagine, I spent a good portion of my life with severe trust issues and was formally diagnosed with PTSD. I had a tough time making friends and told outrageous lies as a defense mechanism against insecurities and low self-esteem. I felt that people couldn't possibly accept or like me because I didn't even like me! But if you give in to others' demons, your abusers win, and have the power to continue to control you, especially if you set the cycle of subconscious feed loops in your head to repeat.

Fear can be divided into two types: acute fear, which is an immediate response to an identifiable threat, and chronic fear, which is long-term and may not be tied to any identifiable source, or perhaps, is rooted in anxiety. While acute fear can be helpful in preventing us from taking stupid risks, chronic fear can lead to long-term mental and physical health issues that include, but aren't limited to, generalized anxiety, obsessive-compulsive disorders, high blood pressure, migraine headaches, dizziness, nausea, etc.

MK-Ultra was a covert, illegal US human research program run by the Central Intelligence Agency's (CIA) Scientific Intelligence Division from the 1950s to the 1970s. MK-Ultra took the idea and feeling of fear to a whole new level. The purpose of the project was to develop drugs, biological weapons, and special tactics that might be useful in interrogations and torture, forced confessions, or involuntary/amnesic assassinations through mind control.

The program involved numerous experiments on human subjects, mostly without their knowledge or consent. These experiments were typically conducted under the guise of legitimate scientific research at universities, hospitals, prisons, schools, mental health institutions, foster homes, and at pharmaceutical companies. The project was first brought to the public's attention in 1975 through investigations by the Church Committee and a presidential commission known as the Rockefeller Commission.

My grandmother once remarked that she found my mother's diagnosis confusing because paranoid schizophrenia, she was told, has a genetic predisposition, and as far as she was aware, the illness didn't run in either side of the family. My mother had also suffered a head injury in a car accident when she was sixteen, one that left her in a short coma during the late 1950s. Nobody in the medical community ever investigated a possible link to a traumatic brain injury.

When my uncle tried to have my mother released from the Tiffin State Hospital, he was told no. She'd already spent eighteen months in confinement. Whether my mom was a victim of MK-Ultra, we'll never know. Years later, she claimed she was the victim of a governmental experiment and coverup, but her diagnosis alone discredited those claims. Her medical records disappeared along with most of the history of the hospital.

The MK-Ultra experiments involved a wide range of drugs, hypnosis, sensory deprivation, isolation, verbal abuse, electroconvulsive shock therapy, and sexual abuse, as well as other forms of psychological and physical torture. Perhaps the most notorious aspect of the MK-Ultra program involved the administration of extraordinary levels of LSD doses (lysergic acid diethylamide), a powerful hallucinogen, to unwitting subjects. This included CIA employees, military personnel, doctors, other government agents, prostitutes, the mentally ill, minorities, soldiers, foster children, the intellectually disabled, and unwitting members of the public, to study their reactions.

Due to its covert nature, the full extent and details of the MK-Ultra program are not completely known or available—and some of it remains classified. Most official records were destroyed in 1973 on the order of then-CIA director Richard Helms. Surviving documents and victim testimonies reveal a research program that relied heavily on inducing fear in its pursuit of mind control techniques.

The CIA's MK-Ultra program played on human fears in several ways:

- **Mind Control**: MK-Ultra sought to explore and develop techniques for mind control and behavioral manipulation. By studying the effects of various substances and methods on human subjects, the program aimed to identify ways to control and influence people's thoughts, emotions, and behaviors. This tapped into the fear of losing control over one's own mind and actions, which is a fundamental fear shared by many individuals.

- **Brainwashing and Interrogation**: Another aspect of MK-Ultra involved researching methods of interrogation, coercion, and brainwashing. This aspect played on the fear of being manipulated or coerced into divulging sensitive information or betraying one's own beliefs. By studying these techniques, the program aimed to exploit and amplify human fears related to interrogation and control.

- **LSD and Other Substances**: MK-Ultra extensively experimented with various substances, including LSD, as a means of achieving mind control and altering individuals' mental states. This aspect of the program played on fears of the unknown and the potential for substances to induce uncontrollable psychological effects. It exploited the fear of losing one's sanity or being subjected to unknown and unpredictable influences.

- **Informed Consent and Ethical Concerns**: One of the most unsettling aspects of MK-Ultra was the lack of informed consent given by the human subjects involved in the experiments. Many participants were unaware that they were being subjected to mind-altering substances or psychological manipulation. This aspect played on the fear of being deceived and used for nefarious purposes, highlighting concerns about ethical boundaries and the potential for abuse of power.

Overall, the MK-Ultra program capitalized on fundamental human fears related to losing control or security, manipulation, and the violation of personal autonomy. By exploring these areas, the program aimed to develop techniques and strategies that could exploit and amplify these fears for strategic, tactical, or intelligence purposes.

Without CIA interference, here are some ways everyday fear may impact our lives:

• **Physiological impact:** The immediate impact of fear is physical. Our heart rate and blood pressure increase. We may start to sweat. Our pupils dilate to let in more light, improving our vision. These changes equip us to deal with immediate threats but can also be damaging if they persist over time, for example, due to chronic stress or anxiety.

• **Cognitive impact:** Fear can impact our decision-making and problem-solving abilities. In some cases, it can sharpen these abilities, allowing us to make quick decisions in response to immediate threats. However, in other cases, fear can cloud our judgment, leading us to make irrational decisions. Over time, chronic fear can lead to mental health issues like depression and anxiety.

• **Behavioral impact:** Fear often leads to changes in behavior. It can make us avoid certain situations or people, limit our activities, or even lead to phobias.

• **Social impact:** Fear can impact our relationships and interactions with others. If we're afraid, we might isolate ourselves or become overly reliant on others for protection and reassurance. On a larger scale, fear can be manipulated to influence societal behavior, as we've seen throughout history in instances of fear-based political propaganda.

• **Impact on personal development:** Fear limits personal growth. If we always avoid situations that frighten us, we might miss out on valuable experiences and opportunities for growth. Overcoming our fears is a source of great personal development.

Healthy fear during life-threatening situations is completely normal. It is a complex and fundamental part of human life, playing a significant role in survival, behavior, and overall mental health. While fear can have negative impacts, particularly if it becomes chronic or is not managed effectively, it can also drive our growth and change. Cognitive-behavioral therapy (CBT), exposure ("desensitization" therapy), or talk therapy and support groups, have been effective in helping some people manage or overcome their fears. And sometimes, the simple act of asking yourself, *"Am I okay at this moment?"*, is enough to lower lesser levels of fear.

Strategies for Managing and Overcoming Fear

Some strategies I, and others I know, have tried, and what we were told:

- **Understanding Fear:** The first step in managing and overcoming fear is understanding it. It's crucial to recognize what triggers your fear and how your body and mind respond to these triggers.

- **Mindfulness and Meditation:** These techniques can help reduce anxiety and fear. By focusing on the present moment, you can avoid becoming consumed with future uncertainties or past experiences. Meditation also helps you to develop a greater understanding of your feelings and thoughts.

- **Breathing Exercises:** When you're fearful, your body can go into fight-or-flight mode. Deep breathing exercises can help calm this response and reduce fear-induced anxiety.

- **Progressive Desensitization:** If your fear is related

to a specific thing or situation (a phobia), a psychological approach known as progressive desensitization or exposure therapy might be beneficial. This involves *gradually* and repeatedly exposing yourself to the thing that frightens you to diminish your fear response.

• **Cognitive Behavioral Therapy (CBT):** CBT is a type of psychotherapy that can help you understand and change thought patterns leading to harmful behaviors or distressing feelings. With this therapy, you can learn to recognize and change thought patterns that lead to fear.

• **Healthy Lifestyle:** Regular exercise, a healthy diet, and adequate sleep can boost your resilience to fear and anxiety. Avoiding caffeine and alcohol, which can trigger anxiety and panic attacks, can also be beneficial.

• **Support Network:** Share your fears with people you trust—friends, family, or a professional counselor. They can provide understanding, advice, and a new perspective. (Thank you, family & friends!)

• **Medication:** In some severe cases, medication may be necessary to manage fear and high anxiety. It's important to discuss this option with a healthcare professional who can provide guidance based on your specific situation and overall health.

• **Positive Visualization:** Visualizing positive outcomes can help reduce fear and anxiety. When fear arises, try to visualize yourself handling the situation effectively and achieving a positive outcome.

Self-Care Practices: Engaging in regular self-care practices, such as taking time for relaxation and recreational activities, helps reduce overall fear and anxiety levels. Hot baths, massage therapy, stretch labs, a walk, or sometimes sitting in the park is enough to add harmony back into your being.

Queen Latifah: Queen Latifah has long stood as one of my most cherished actors. Her performances inspired me in a deeply personal way. Her roles often depict powerful women, embodying a perfect blend of bravery, humor, and vulnerability. These characters are fearless, or at least they wield the strength to face and conquer the fears that confront them, transforming them into symbols of success. As a young adult, I found myself drawn to Queen Latifah's spirit, to the point where I secretly wished we were sisters. Her on-screen persona exuded a courage I desperately wanted to emulate. It was more than mere acting; it was a statement, a guide, an inspiration. Sometimes streaming a good movie can be a balm to your soul. Characters and their carriage speak to us, reminding us that to conquer fear is to understand that there will be failures.

Remember, it's normal to experience fear, and it's okay to seek help if your fear feels overwhelming. If fear is affecting your daily life, please seek professional help.

Integrity – The Cornerstone of Character

"Integrity has no need of rules."
—Albert Camus

Before marrying my husband, our relationship reached a critical point around year one. We both had experienced turbulent marriages with incompatible partners, leaving us feeling a bit unbalanced. I had some shortcomings to consider, too, and when you're as prideful as I was, this was difficult. Our insecurities and my immaturity played a significant role in this impasse. At that moment, my husband-to-be questioned my integrity, which offended me. He suggested breaking up, assuming our core values were too disparate. Frustrated, we retreated to separate rooms, seething with anger.

During this heated situation, I pondered the concept of integrity. Did I possess any? What exactly were core values? Unbeknownst to my beloved, I compiled a list of what I believed were my core values. Meanwhile, he was doing the same in the adjacent room. To our surprise, when we compared our lists, they were remarkably similar! This revelation sparked numerous discussions about our future together and how we might navigate our personality differences. We acknowledged the importance of mutual respect and the need for occasional personal space in managing these differences with love—and this, for us, meant building an *interdependent* partnership on a foundation of integrity.

Interdependence emphasizes the interconnectedness of a relationship and promotes an understanding of one's partner that goes beyond isolated identities. It encourages independence with hobbies and/or friends, or alone time *and* time spent together. We don't exercise control over one another. We make no *demands* upon each other. We can spend time apart, with other people, without getting angry or feeling insecure or threatened. I trust my husband and he trusts me. Infidelity, we mutually decided, brings no added value to our partnership. When we reunite, we always have interesting things to discuss—and yes, we share plenty of intimacy, time, and mutual interests, too.

Integrity is the quality of being honest and ethical, and having strong core values. It involves consistently adhering to your defined set of values and behaving in a trustworthy and honorable manner—even when others can't hear you or aren't looking. A person with intact and healthy integrity acts with honor and demonstrates sincerity and reliability. Integrity also implies a sense of completeness, unity, and wholeness in one's character. I now consider its exercise a sort of sacred ritual in my life, one that deeply contributes to my inner peace. In my early years, I struggled with integrity. Trauma had profound impacts on my sense of self and my ability to generate consistent integrity.

Here are a few reasons trauma victims typically struggle with integrity:

- **Trust issues**: Trauma often shatters a person's trust in others, leading to difficulties in forming and maintaining healthy relationships. This mistrust makes it challenging to engage in open and honest communication, which is essential for maintaining integrity.

• **Emotional dysregulation**: Trauma usually disrupts the normal functioning of the nervous system, leading to heightened states of anxiety, fear, or anger (the fight-or-flight response). Such intense emotions make it difficult for victims to act in alignment with their values, as they may find it challenging to effectively manage and regulate their emotions.

• **Self-blame and shame**: Trauma victims typically internalize feelings of guilt, shame, or self-blame, believing they are solely responsible for any traumatic event or its consequences, that everything is their fault or is part of a serious character flaw absent in "*normal*" people. This self-blame erodes a person's self-worth and makes it harder for them to act in ways that align with their core values.

• **Coping mechanisms**: Trauma leads many individuals to develop coping mechanisms that compromise their integrity. For example, someone may resort to self-destructive behaviors, substance abuse, promiscuity, risky behavior, or deception to numb pain or gain a sense of control. These coping strategies often undermine their ability to act with integrity.

• **Fragmented sense of self**: Trauma may fragment a person's sense of self and lead to feelings of dissociation or identity confusion, which is what happened to me. This fragmentation makes it challenging to have a consistent and integrated set of values, as the trauma victim struggles to define who they are and what they stand for.

It's important to note that struggling with integrity does not mean trauma victims lack the ability to develop integrity or are somehow irreparably flawed. Trauma is a complex and deeply impactful experience. The healing process involves addressing these challenges and working toward reintegrating both a sense of integrity and self-worth. Professional support, such as therapy, plays a crucial role in helping trauma survivors navigate these struggles and restore a sense of integrity in their lives.

The Significance of Core Values

Core values are guiding stars in our lives. They influence our actions, shape our behavior, and set the tone for how we interact with the world around us. They stem from the depths of our beliefs, lessons learned, and experiences lived. These values are unique for every individual, making each of us a distinct masterpiece of the universe.

Personal values are the pillars that uphold our decisions and judgments, giving us the strength to stand firm during our most challenging moments. Moral codes guide us when we are lost, and they provide a sense of clarity when things seem hazy. When you learn what matters most to you, making choices becomes easier and more meaningful, even if others around you don't or won't accept or understand. Staying true to yourself and on your personal path of enrichment, spirituality, and health is found in the bedrock of the core values you develop—and it's never too late to pour your foundation!

Understanding Your Core Values

To comprehend your values, you must introspect. Ask

yourself hard questions—what truly matters to you? What makes you happy? What gives your life purpose? During which moments do you like yourself best? The answers to these questions are a starting point for understanding your personal values.

For instance, if relationships and family make you happy, perhaps *love* and *connection* are among your core values. If fighting for justice fires up your spirit, perhaps *fairness* and *equality* is essential to you. If helping others feel better jazzes you, maybe *service* is your calling and a core value. Understanding your values requires honesty, courage, and self-awareness. It is a continuous process that evolves as we grow, learn, and experience different phases of life.

Upholding Integrity

Integrity is often defined as doing the right thing, even when no one is watching. It is a quality that intertwines like DNA around your personal values. Upholding integrity means living in alignment with your values, remaining consistent in your words and actions, and staying true to yourself and being true to others, even in the face of pressure or temptation.

While personal values provide a direction, integrity is the unwavering commitment to follow that direction despite hurdles and challenges.

Integrity is about accepting responsibility for your actions, being accountable, apologizing when you're wrong, and making amends when necessary. It is about maintaining honesty, transparency, and authenticity in your endeavors. But it is also realizing you're human, and as a human, complete perfection isn't possible. So, integrity also means getting up again if you fall. Also, be compassionate with yourself. It helps you continue a positive path.

. . .

Why Integrity Matters

Integrity helps us build trust in our relationships, create a positive image in our professional lives, and maintain self-esteem. It fortifies our character, making us reliable, respectable, and powerfully influential in our sphere of life.

With integrity, we can confidently look at ourselves in the mirror, knowing we have lived a day in line with our personal values. Without it, sure, we might achieve success or fool someone, but it will usually be devoid of fulfillment or contentment —and eventually, there are consequences. I've witnessed this countless times. I live near one of the most affluent zip codes on the planet, a winter playground for the exceedingly financially blessed. Despite this excess wealth and the ability to do whatever they please, buy anything they want, or travel anywhere on the planet, people often confide to me their loneliness, boredom, lack of purpose, the reticent abuse they endure, or marital disenchantment. And some of them end up in jail for alleged Ponzi schemes or fraud.

The happiest people I know strike a balance between their joy and responsibilities, and simply choose to love and feel joy regardless of their wealth or lack of. They serve others without resentment, don't seek out accolades or attention, but instead, tend valuable relationships, and engage in self-care.

Max is an example for me of this unbound love wrapped up in integrity:

The warm ambiance of a mutual friend's birthday dinner was punctuated by laughter and soft music. I found myself sitting between my husband and a man I'd never met—Max. Max is an Iranian émigré, a successful businessman, and an indefatigable lover of life.

As the evening unraveled, I was drawn toward Max's humble charisma. Max makes you feel as if you're the only one in a room who matters, but to him, everyone matters. His attentiveness was manifested when he reminded the waiter about the forgotten soup I'd ordered. Max pays attention—to everything, as if he's witnessing it for the first time.

Max and I freely conversed, traversing topics from philosophy to Persian poetry. Max possessed an intense depth that was as enchanting as it was mysterious. His stories of growing up in Iran, escaping political persecution, and building a new life in the US filled me with awe.

By the time dessert was served, I found myself captivated. My feelings were not romantic or untoward, but rather a deep admiration and respect. Seeing him arrive alone, I inquired about his personal life. Surely, this man had a remarkable wife. His eyes softened as he revealed his status as a widower. He focused most of his energy, he said, on his daughters and grandson.

A few days later, I accepted his invitation for tea at his Persian rug gallery. There, amid an array of beautifully woven tapestries, Max unraveled his perspective on life. He pointed out the unique mandala-like designs on the rugs, explaining that they represented God's grandeur from a unique vantage point —"as above, so below." To me, it was spirituality from a mathematical perspective, a geometric weaving of fractals, a microcosm of the cosmos representing unity, harmony, and love.

As we sipped our tea, Max opened the world of Rumi to me, and said, "The most important thing we can do is love." Like the men I'd mysteriously met at the Boynton Vortex in Sedona, Max emphasized how love is the paramount force in our lives, the healer of all wounds, the bridge that unites us all. God, I was convinced, was trying to tell me something...again and again. I was beginning to get the message.

Growing up in Ohio, I had been taught to view Iranians through a lens of suspicion and fear. But here was Max, the antithesis of those misguided stereotypes. His authentic compassion, combined with an acceptance that never faltered, moved me deeply. It occurred to me then how Max exemplified a core belief I held: religion, careers, money, big houses, cars, or nationality didn't define us, our actions did. He was the embodiment of love and acceptance I had seldom seen in action.

Like a mirror held up to the world, Max is a lighthouse guiding others through and into love. He is also unassuming, honest, and generous in his dealings. His energy is magnetic, drawing people toward him, inspiring them to embrace love as he does—with unreserved joy.

A Journey Toward Personal Fulfillment

Understanding your personal values and upholding integrity is a lifelong journey, a path paved with challenges, self-discovery, and personal fulfillment. This journey requires introspection, self-awareness, and the courage to face our inner selves. It demands patience, for understanding our core values is not an overnight process, but a gradual discovery that unfolds with each life experience.

Once we understand and embrace our values, upholding integrity becomes our commitment to staying true to these values. It becomes our personal GPS system that guides us through life's twists and turns, leading us toward a life of authenticity, fulfillment, and happiness. For when you understand your values and live with integrity, you are not just existing, but truly living, the way Max does.

Credibility – Building Trust and Respect

"If you believe that the greatest challenge you've got is credibility, then the way you get that is you earn it, right? That's not something that any set of policymakers can bestow."
—Joe Kennedy III

In our cyber unreality of "Selfie-And-Filter," where followers are considered mightier than swords, hordes of people seem to believe that reaching influencer status is the pinnacle of human achievement. In this illusory realm of social media, credibility appears to be an outdated relic, left forgotten and neglected in the hard drives of people's hearts. Credibility often feels replaced by a quest for follower counts, the perfect aesthetic, virtual power, or trendy hashtags—and social media in its myriad forms is typically corrupted with misinformation, propaganda, and lies. Yet occasionally, there exist nuggets of wisdom, innovation, grand memories, and deep friendships outside its vitriolic algorithms.

As a child, I took up the hobby of manufacturing lies. It

began innocently enough: a yes here, a no there, all to shield adults from my abuse, which was, in my naïve mind, surely my fault. I was an apprentice in the art of truth-concealing and anger-suppressing, two skills that promised dire consequences if not mastered. Every adult I knew lied—to me, to others, but mostly, to themselves.

As I grew, lying became my magic carpet, swiftly whisking me away from awkward encounters or emotional distress. My lies were like ill-timed jokes, distracting from any immediate tensions but far from contributing to my self-esteem. Yet, each lie I told was like a personal ghost, invisible but haunting. Whether it was fanciful tales about my picture-perfect family, embellishing my academic achievements, or the classic "I'm sick" excuse to skip work, I only deceived my most critical audience member—myself. I might have tricked others occasionally, particularly under the effects of some strong spirits or mind-altering substances, but the curtain call always came sooner than I liked, revealing my charade. Because let's face it, people aren't always as gullible as we hope or want them to be. My web of lies, woven so meticulously, ended up pricking more than my finger.

I view lies like termites. The big ones take down your foundation of credibility in a single fell swoop. And the little ones? They slowly nibble away, unveiling a tortured soul of dysfunction. That said, some lies are necessary, a forgivable wink in the cosmic order of things. These are the lies that might save a life, prevent harm, or simply shield another's feelings. In a strange twist of fate, such lies often uplift our credibility rather than lower it—and lying, I've learned, is just as much a part of the human condition as truth-telling—whether we want to admit it or not.

It's ironic to me that credibility doesn't fall from the sky, but rather, rises like a phoenix, from the ashes of past indiscretions and mistakes—and can be learned. In the end, becoming a person of credence felt far more rewarding than my previous dips into shallow superficiality. But it took years and I'm still a work in progress. Credibility, I've slowly discovered, is the real "influencer."

On a planet where words are as plentiful as the air we breathe, credibility is a rare gold standard of communication. It is the cornerstone of effective leadership, the pillar upon which relationships are built, and it is a currency that can elevate your personal and professional life.

Defining Credibility

Credibility is derived from the Latin word *credibilis*, which means "worthy of belief." It is the quality of being trusted, believed in, and respected. It's a characteristic defined not by what we say about ourselves, but by what *others* say and think about us.

Imagine a seed. Buried beneath the soil, it remains unseen, yet with proper care and nurturing, it emerges as a plant that eventually bears fruit or flowers. Our credibility is like that seed. Initially invisible, it grows over time, through our words and actions. Credibility becomes a powerful testament to our character. I try not to let mine wither anymore.

Credibility in Personal Life

Credibility is foundational to all personal relationships. It's not just about honesty; it's also about consistency, reliability, and trustworthiness.

In friendships, credibility translates to being someone your friends can trust and rely upon. It means keeping your word, showing up when needed, and being the same person in both private and public settings. In romantic relationships, credibility manifests as emotional honesty and respectful communication.

The credibility you cultivate in your personal life lays the groundwork for self-respect and self-trust. As you consistently act in ways that reflect your celestial, elevated, higher plane values, and beliefs, you strengthen your self-esteem, boost your confidence, and nurture your mental and emotional well-being.

Credibility in Professional Life

In the professional arena, credibility is your invisible passport to success. It's not about winning one-time deals or impressing superiors with flashy presentations; it's about establishing a track record of competence, accountability, and dependability.

Credibility on the job means delivering high-quality work, owning your mistakes, and learning from them, respecting deadlines, and maintaining professionalism in all interactions. It means "walking the talk," leading by example, and creating an environment of trust and mutual respect.

Credible professionals value teamwork, innovation, and service. They consistently demonstrate these values through their actions. Sages are the ones who are trusted with important tasks and considered for leadership roles, and whose opinion is sought.

Cultivating Credibility

Credibility, I learned, is not a one-time achievement but a lifelong pursuit. It begins with self-awareness and honesty about who you are, what you stand for, and where your strengths and weaknesses lie. It continues with intentional actions that align with your values and commitments.

Here are a few key steps to building and maintaining credibility:

- **Consistency:** Be consistent in your actions, whether

big or small. The way you manage your commitments, interact with others, and respond to challenges speaks volumes about your credibility.

- **Honesty:** Speak truthfully, even when it's uncomfortable. Honesty earns respect and trust, forming a solid base for credibility.

- **Accountability:** Take responsibility for your actions and decisions. When you make a mistake, own it, learn from it, and make amends if necessary.

- **Reliability:** Follow through on your promises. If you commit to doing something, ensure you do it. Reliability reinforces others' belief in your competence and dependability.

- **Respectfulness:** Treat everyone with respect and kindness, irrespective of their status or role. Respectfulness shows that you value people, reinforcing your personal and professional credibility.

Credibility, whether in personal or professional life, cannot be bought or faked; it must be earned. It's not always easy, and it requires time and commitment, but its rewards are significant. With credibility, you gain trust, respect, and influence, and you set the stage for fulfilling relationships and lasting success.

Value – The Measure of Your Self-Worth

"No one can make you feel inferior without your consent."
—Eleanor Roosevelt

During a time of socio-economic desperation and an array of poor personal choices, I found myself employed as a stripper in an upscale club on the outskirts of Cleveland. It was a chapter of my life defined by reckless decisions, one of which was a passionate, illicit affair with a married man.

By age twenty-three, I was pregnant and alone, the father of my child having returned to his wife. Presented with difficult choices—adoption, abortion, or raising the child myself—I chose to keep my baby. My path, already strewn with hardship, was made even more difficult by this decision. A pregnant single mom, at this time, was considered a disgrace. Charity or kindness was scarce but the shaming labels I received were plentiful. Additionally, my child's father warned me to stay away from him and his community, under the threat of being rolled up in a rug and thrown into a landfill.

During a slow Thursday shift at the club, I met a man named Joe, freshly released from prison. He wore a pale blue velour sweatsuit—and a gold pinky ring. He had eyes for my friend Gwen, so I introduced them and stepped aside—my gesture of goodwill in an otherwise cutthroat world. I had a drink at the bar and ruminated over my skill as a third wheel.

Not long after, I found myself summoned to the cordoned-off VIP section. I was escorted by a duo of suited men to where Joe was seated. However, he wasn't interested in a dance. Instead, he beckoned me to take a seat, his eyes filled with curiosity. He inquired about my real name and sought to understand my reasons for working in a strip club. He said I didn't quite fit in here. In response, I shared with him the truth of my situation: I was a single mother, struggling to raise a young son.

"Is the child's father contributing?" he probed further.

I shook my head.

"Does his wife know?"

"No," I said.

"What's his name?" he asked.

I hesitated. "Nothing worse than a rat," I said.

Joe nodded in understanding, remarking, "Mistakes, big or small, are part of our journey... What truly matters is our ability to learn from them. In my view, a man who fails to support his offspring is far worse than any rat."

As he reclined in his chair, his gaze upon me turned analytical. "Are you attending the Feast of the Assumption this weekend?" he asked.

I revealed that my child's father had forbidden me from setting foot on Murray Hill. Yet again, he insisted on knowing the man's name. This time, I told him. A moment of recognition flickered across his face as he reached into his sweatsuit pocket. "I know dat guy." It was all he said. Pulling out a hefty roll of cash bound by a rubber band, he handed me a generous sum. Joe said he admired the decency I had shown in giving my friend a chance to earn some money. He asked about my next shift.

"I work a day shift tomorrow," I said.

"What time you off?" he asked.

"Seven," I answered.

I was left bewildered, not expecting such a generous transaction without having to dance. On Friday evening, my friend Priscilla burst into the dressing room, yelling enthusiastically about a limousine waiting outside—with instructions to ferry me and two friends to the Feast of the Assumption. "And I'm one of your friends!" Pricilla exclaimed.

Despite the initial confusion, we found ourselves comfortably seated in the grand vehicle.

When we reached Murray Hill, the thick throng of people seemed like an impenetrable barrier, kept in check by a phalanx of police officers. To my astonishment, the police stepped aside, creating a path for our limo. Upon arrival at the R bar, an awaiting man directed my friends to enjoy a meal courtesy of "Joe Loose," while I was led into a large private dining hall filled with about sixty other men seated at round tables draped in white linen.

There, at the head of the room, at the only long table, sat Joe, playing the role of master of ceremonies. With a wave of his hand, he commanded a place by his side, slapping another man alongside his head and telling the guy to find another seat. When I took my place beside Joe amidst the unfamiliar faces, he rose to offer a toast.

"I'd like to propose a toast," he said. He held up his glass. "Every one of you mother fuckers better stand up, right now!"

Everyone did.

"This here's a classy lady, a real tomato, and she will be treated as such," he said. "From this day forth, B.A. is *ALWAYS* welcome in Little Italy, capiche? To B.A.!"

"To B.A.!"

Joe leaned over where I sat stunned. "How'd I do, kid?" He winked at me.

Breathlessly, I whispered, "You did just fine, Joe."

He sat down, patted my knee, and we proceeded to eat dinner, with me being the *ONLY* woman in the room.

From then on, my life took a turn. I no longer danced at the strip club. Instead, I found myself waitressing for private craps games in Murray Hill, a stint that came to a tragic end the day my two-year-old son disappeared. Upon one of Joe's men finding my son safe and sound at a nearby park, relief washed over me, mirrored by the apprehension on Joe's face.

"You're fired," he said.

I sobbed in protest. He handed me a kerchief and I dabbed my eyes.

"Listen, kid," he began, his voice steady and strong. "You possess too many smarts to be some guy's tomato. The men around here, including me, we're all flawed in our ways... and if you stick around, there are only three outcomes for your kid: prison, death, or a combination of both. Get the hell out of here, go back to school, and build a better future for you and Joey. Trust me, you'll be fine."

That was the last time I saw Joe. As ludicrous as it may sound today, I was never sure who he really was or what he did. I kept my mouth shut and didn't ask. Google searches didn't yet exist. Sure, people talked. But not too much around me.

My connection to Joe was never romantic. It was a paternal friendship. Perhaps Joe felt I had been dealt a tough hand as a former foster kid, ward of the court and single mom. Maybe he thought he could redeem himself and his sins through saving me. Regardless of his motives, Joe recognized something valuable in me that, at the time, I couldn't see in myself.

He gave me financial help, true, but he also offered me an unexpected sense of safety and reciprocity I'd never known. Joe extended a hand in friendship during a weighty moment of my vulnerability. In a surprising twist, his dismissal of me was a lifeline, a push toward a better future—and he was saying, "You've got this!" He encouraged me to pursue something higher than he had, to escape the confines of a limited mind.

The mysterious *Joe Loose,* I learned after he died, had once been a notorious figure, an active participant in the dark underbelly of Cleveland, Ohio's notorious Italian crime family. He was involved, I also read, in illicit activities, from burglary and other crimes, to leading a reformation of the "*family*" after a series of federal indictments. This dangerous and elusive figure whom everyone feared had shown me kindness that was hard for most others to comprehend. I was later told he was violent and brutal. I never witnessed this part of Joe. He was nicknamed *Joe Loose* for a reason, people said. They insisted the man had a screw loose in his head. This wasn't my experience. I knew a gentle and redeeming side of Joe Loose he rarely showed to others.

Despite his criminal background, Joe taught me about integrity, loyalty, and the importance of rising above one's circumstances. He didn't sugarcoat his life; he acknowledged his mistakes and learned from them. I also think he had moments when they weighed heavily. Through his actions, he encouraged me to do the same—to strive for something better—and to be better. He was a complex figure, a paradox in himself. A man of his status, encrusted in a world of crime and depravity, which sometimes included gruesome murders, had shown me an unanticipated respect that few others had.

In the end, Joe reminded me that it's never too late to change your path, to strive for something better, and to prioritize my child's safety and well-being above all else. Joe's story may have been etched with mistakes, but his legacy lives on in me—a single mother he believed in and empowered. He showed me the measure of my worth and the power of a second chance, and for that, I will always be grateful. His influence helped me understand that everyone, no matter their circumstances, has intrinsic value, and sometimes, all it takes is one person to see that value and foster its growth.

In an era wherein societal norms, social media, materialism, money, media, and medicine often dictate our self-perception, recognizing our self-worth may seem like a daunting task. Yet it is in this very recognition that we unearth the bedrock of our self-esteem, confidence, and resilience. We embark on the profound journey of embracing our true value, independent of external factors.

Understanding Self-Worth

Self-worth is the intrinsic understanding and acknowledgment of your value as a human being. It is the deep-seated belief in your own worthiness and dignity, regardless of your circumstances, accomplishments, wealth, status, or physical attributes.

Societal standards, the internet's echo chambers, material possessions, financial status, popular media, and sometimes even our age, looks, and health are often seen as measures of our worth. But true self-worth lies beyond these transient, illusory, and external factors. It springs from our character, our compassion, our courage, and our authenticity—the essence of who we are. So, who are *YOU*?

The Pitfalls of External Validation

When we tether our self-worth to external validation, we construct a shaky foundation for our inner security and self-esteem. As we seek approval and praise from others, our sense of self-worth becomes susceptible to their judgments and opinions. Every social media like, every dollar earned, every material possession acquired, every media image emulated, and every health standard met or unmet, every hand clap, becomes an inaccurate and fleeting measure of our worthiness.

These external factors are not true indicators of our personal worth. They are unpredictable illusions beyond our control. Just as fast as they fling us to the heights of grandiosity, they can just as easily plummet us into a sense of inadequacy, anxiety, restlessness, or dissatisfaction. It is crucial to disentangle self-worth from these illusions. As a human being, you're too valuable!

Jealousy, resentment, bragging, and insecurity are potent emotions that can hijack your personal worth, too. These unpleasant emotions typically arise from unaddressed childhood trauma, negative experiences, unlearned coping and communication skills, intrusive thoughts, or interpersonal dynamics. Understanding your personal psychological roots of these feelings is crucial for fostering healthier relationships and emotional stability:

1. Jealousy:

Jealousy is a multifaceted emotion, often elicited when a person perceives a threat to a valued relationship or their sense of self-worth. Jealousy can rear over something as simple as a colleague receiving a well-deserved promotion or as harsh as discovering your spouse has a lover. Psychologically, it roots from several personal factors:

- **Insecurity:** This is a primary driver of jealousy. A person with low self-esteem or feelings of unworthiness typically feels threatened by others he or she perceives as more attractive, competent, or successful.

- **Fear of loss:** Fear of losing a cherished relationship or the love of someone important can fuel jealousy.

• **Lack of trust:** Trust issues, either from past experiences or existing relationship dynamics, can intensify feelings of jealousy.

2. Resentment:

Resentment is a feeling of persistent bitterness or indignation at having been treated unfairly. The personal psychological roots of resentment include:

• **Perceived injustice:** If an individual perceives that he or she has been wronged without appropriate rectification, injustice can lead to harboring resentment.

• **Unmet expectations:** When personal expectations in relationships or life scenarios are not met, and these expectations are perceived to be reasonable, resentment can develop.

• **Lack of forgiveness:** Holding on to past wrongs and not allowing oneself to forgive can perpetuate feelings of resentment.

3. Insecurity:

Insecurity is the state of feeling uncertain, anxious, or inadequate. It typically originates
from:

• **Negative past experiences:** Early life experiences, particularly those involving criticism, rejection, or failure, can plant seeds of insecurity.

- **Poor self-image:** Low self-esteem and negative self-perceptions often go together with insecurity.

- **Uncertainty about the future:** Fear of the unknown, particularly in aspects like career progression, financial stability, or romantic relationships, can trigger insecurity.

- **Comparisons:** When we measure ourselves against others, we often only see their highlights without considering their unseen struggles or unique advantages that might have contributed to their successes. This may foster feelings of inadequacy that detracts from our unique qualities and accomplishments. Comparisons leave us stuck in a never-ending loop of dissatisfaction, where contentment remains perpetually out of reach.

In many cases, these emotions are intertwined, with one feeding into and off of the other. For example, insecurity leads to jealousy in relationships, and resentment over perceived inequities. Likewise, prolonged feelings of jealousy and resentment often deepen feelings of insecurity.

Understanding the roots of these painful emotions is the first step toward addressing and managing them. Therapeutic approaches help individuals reframe negative thought patterns that fuel these emotions. Additionally, fostering a positive self-image, learning to trust, setting realistic expectations, practicing forgiveness, and building resilience can aid in mitigating jealousy, resentment, and insecurity.

Cultivating a Healthy Sense of Self-Worth

Cultivating a healthy sense of self-worth involves recognizing our personal value and nurturing our self-esteem. Here are a few steps to guide you on this transformative safari:

- **Self-Awareness:** Start by exploring your inner self. Like Joe Loose, understand your strengths, acknowledge your weaknesses, celebrate your achievements, and accept your failures (and the consequences). Recognize the qualities that make you unique and valuable, list them if you must—and start there.

- **Self-Compassion:** Be gentle with yourself. Treat yourself with the same kindness, patience, and understanding you would extend to a dear friend or treasured family member. Self-compassion helps silence your inner critic and encourages you, instead, to focus upon and acknowledge your worth.

- **Mindfulness:** Practice mindfulness. Being present allows you to appreciate yourself in the here and now, without the distortions of past regrets or future anxieties. It fosters a balanced perspective of yourself. If you feel anxious or stressed, ask yourself, "Am I okay at this moment?" Usually, you will discover, that you are okay at this moment.

Thich Nhat Hanh, by extension, taught me a lesson about mindfulness that I call, **"Peeling the Mandarin"**:

When I feel restless, I grab a mandarin orange and sit with it. I admire its color and texture before I peel. I toss and roll it between my palms. I think about what the universe or God put into this mandarin for it to arrive at my home. I look for the seed, the tree, the roots, the sun, air, water, stars, and the galaxies to which this mandarin is connected.

I slowly peel the mandarin orange. The skin is initially semi-tough, but I manage to pierce it with a fingernail. Soon, I separate the peel from the fruit. Its vibrant color and citrus scent fill the space around me. I gently detach each segment. I think of nothing else but the mandarin. I focus on its color, smell, the feel of its lightly dimpled skin against my fingertips, and the sweet juice that eventually cools my tongue when I pop a section into my mouth. I consider the health, light, and energy this fruit provides to my blood, bones, cells, and brain.

Living in the present moment, fully immersed in the task at hand, and appreciating the senses it triggers, without judgment or wandering thoughts, is mindfulness. Nothing else exists in that moment.

The sense of peace I experience over such a simple act allows me to quiet my mind, slow down, and savor both the interaction and transformation. Just as the mandarin transformed gradually from seed to tree to fruit, so too, our lives, from fetus, to infant, toddler, adolescent, and then adult. Our success depends not on our materialism but our emotional and spiritual health, and this ability to transition, to pivot and to grow. And for me, it begins again with peeling a mandarin.

- **Affirmations:** Read positive affirmations and stories or listen to the music you love to reinforce your self-worth. Doing things you love, even if it's taking a short walk outside, or listening to your favorite music, or thinking about the happiest moment of your life significantly boosts self-esteem. Sometimes, if I'm feeling low, I read correspondence from others who claim I've helped them or remember kind words or accolades to remind myself a sad state is temporary, and like gas, will pass.

- **Self-Care:** Prioritize self-care. Physical, emotional, and mental well-being are fundamental to a healthy sense of self-worth. Exercise regularly, maintain a balanced diet, rest sufficiently, get massages, take baths, or buy some ice cream! However, if you feel that the level of your pain is beyond self-care, please ask for and seek professional help when needed.

• **Healthy Relationships:** Surround yourself with people who respect and appreciate you for who you are, not for what you have or achieve. Nourishing relationships are key here and should based in sincerity and love, the type of love that greatly enhances your sense of joy and self-worth.

• **Forgiving Yourself:** At times, we can become our harshest critics, magnifying our shortcomings, and neglecting our achievements. Embracing self-forgiveness for our past missteps is a fundamental step on the path toward healing and personal growth.

• **Elevating Self-Confidence:** Set and Achieve Small Goals. Start with manageable goals that are relatively easy to achieve. Each success builds confidence and prepares you for bigger challenges. Learning something new can improve your self-confidence, too. This could be a new language, a musical instrument, a sport, or any skill that interests you. Mine was learning to parallel park in a crowded entertainment district while others watched! And keep in mind too, it is perfectly normal to experience fluctuations in self-confidence.

• **Embracing Failure:** Understand that failure is a part of life and an opportunity for learning and growth. Don't let fear of failure prevent you from taking risks.

• **Positive Relationships:** Surround yourself with positive, supportive people who encourage you and believe in you.

• **Celebrating Your Achievements:** No matter how small they may seem, acknowledging your accomplishments can boost your self-esteem.

- **Practicing Gratitude:** Focusing on what you are grateful for, rather than what you lack, can shift your perspective, and enhance your self-esteem.

- **Laughter:** Humor is an invaluable tool during difficult times. It provides release, relief, and perspective that is healing and unifying. In the face of adversity, a well-timed joke or humorous observation abruptly cuts through tension, fosters a sense of connection, and enhances shared experience. Humor also acts as a mental break, allowing people to reorient perspectives or calm down. It helps build resilience by teaching individuals to view challenges in a more healthy and manageable light. The therapeutic power of laughter has been recognized across cultures, and in times of crisis, humor can be a lifeline, bringing comfort and humanity to stressful situations.

- **Professional Help:** If low self-confidence is significantly impacting your life, consider seeking help from a therapist or counselor. Cognitive behavioral therapy (CBT), for example, can be particularly effective in addressing issues related to self-esteem.

Your worth on this planet is immeasurable. It is not defined by societal standards, social media likes, material possessions, financial status, unrealistic media images, comparisons, or your looks. Your self-worth is in your existence, your humanity, and in the unique value of your experiences, beliefs, and outstanding qualities. You are the guardian angel of your worth. Embrace you, celebrate you, and let yourself serve as a unique and special beacon of light, one that brings you joy but also illuminates the soul and inner peace of others.

Attachment – A Double-Edged Sword

"Attachment to the past and fears concerning the future not only govern the way you select the things you own but also represent the criteria by which you make choices in every aspect of your life, including your relationships with people and your job."
—Marie Kondo

I used to harbor the misconception that my happiness, my social engagements, my personal survival, and my achievements were contingent upon the actions and approval of others—and I was attached to that misconception. I heavily relied on the judgment of others, responding emotively, with a deep-rooted instinct for physical and emotional preservation.

For example, naiveté, fear, and passivity led me to concede more than necessary to others' whims or opinions. I was susceptible to manipulation, becoming intensely dependent on others' approval to feel *normal.* I was inconsistent, often leaning toward impulsivity, not realizing that I was my own stumbling block. I subconsciously waited for others to shoulder my responsibilities because I was ingrained with the belief that I was incapable of taking care of myself—a notion reinforced by the foster system, our political framework, the financial system, social media, relationships, society, patriarchal religion, and workplaces. Basically, if I wasn't rescued by a knight in shining Armani, I was doomed to a life of abject poverty and helplessness. I was taught that my worth in life was to be strictly measured by the status of a husband to whom I might *attach* myself.

My perspective shifted when I recognized that I could modulate my attachments. Previously, my definitions of success and normality were tied to the possession of material items, status, and the illusion of wealth. I chased the shiny and fleeting, mistaking it for personal value. It was an exhausting never-ending cycle, leaving me mentally and physically drained.

As Americans, we are generally the most significant consumers on the planet, often attaching our identities and success to the size of our homes, our professional ratings, our cars, our partners, and our financial standing. We eagerly anticipate the next big innovation to provide the tranquility or peace of mind we seek. When it fails to arrive, we shift our attention to the next new thing. Our attachments expand to people, places, ideologies, and politics, gripping them so firmly that it often contradicts our integrity, core values, and personal beliefs.

Debt, despair, isolation, addiction, and self-glorification have unfortunately become additional attachments. Fortunately, amidst these challenges, we still witness humanity's resilience—the individuals who manage to discard these burdensome attachments, liberating themselves from unhealthy cravings and compulsions. They stand as beacons of hope, illuminating the path to true fulfillment and peace for the rest of us.

. . .

The human experience is always characterized by various paradoxes, and among the most striking of these is the interplay among attachment, freedom, and bondage. On the surface, these three entities appear distinctly separate; however, a deeper understanding reveals how together they are bound, affecting our lives, interactions, and perceptions in substantial ways. To minimize attachment is to discover enriched existence, where freedom is not just a concept, but a lived reality outside of bondage.

Attachment forms the crux of our human experience. From the earliest stages of our lives, we form attachments—to parents, to friends, to objects, ideas, and later, to partners, career paths, and societal constructs. These attachments are perceived as the cord that anchors us in the sea of life, offering security, comfort, and a sense of identity. But there lies its paradox—while attachment fosters a feeling of connection and belonging, it may also breed dependency and bondage, limiting the expansiveness of our individual and collective experiences.

While we all yearn for freedom—the freedom to think, act, feel, and choose—we often find ourselves confined by the attachments we've fostered. Bondage manifests as an inability to live authentically, restricted instead by the fear of losing what we are attached to. The fear of alienation, judgment, failure, or simply the unfamiliar. Bondage creeps into most of our lives subtly, masquerading as comfort, or fame or money or applause, only to leave us shackled in a prison of our own making. We bind ourselves to mortgages, marriage, illness, credit cards, jobs, or family—even if they aren't good for us, because we've become attached—to responsibility, expectation, fear, insecurity, or despair.

To decipher the dynamic of attachment and bondage, we must first understand that the essence of bondage is not in the attachment itself, but in our relationship with the attachment. When we attach our sense of self, our happiness, or our worth to something external, we unwittingly create negative conditions for our freedom. You are not your position or title. You're so much more. And after your position or title ends, so too, its perks. The external entity, be it a person, material possession, or idea, becomes the puppeteer, and we, the puppet, manipulated by the strings of *perceived* need and security.

So, how do we navigate this complex terrain? The answer lies in shifting our perspective on attachment, freedom, and bondage. And it begins with self-awareness. The process of understanding our attachments, identifying those that serve our growth, and recognizing those that limit us, is crucial. This introspection allows us to reevaluate our dependencies, revealing that many of our attachments are not based on necessity, but rather on pre-conditioned beliefs, wants, or fears.

Next is the cultivation of inner security and wholeness. When we find completeness within ourselves, external attachments transform from being sources of validation to channels of joy, connection, and growth. This shift does not mean renouncing material things or people but reshaping our relationship with them, understanding that they complement our lives rather than define them.

Additionally, we must understand that freedom is not the absence of bonds, but the ability to choose and create those that uplift us. It's the freedom to love, risk, fail, and venture into the unknown, unchained. It is through the informed choice of our attachments that we assert our freedom, switching the programming of the negative subconscious beliefs we've integrated.

Finally, the embrace of impermanence plays a vital role in navigating this dynamic, too. Everything changes—people, circumstances, ideas. When we accept this fundamental truth, we learn to hold our attachments lightly. We begin to see that the real bondage is not in forming attachments, but in clinging to the ones that no longer serve us.

Understanding the dynamics of attachment, freedom, and bondage provides an avenue for empowerment. It helps us tread the delicate balance between forming meaningful connections and preserving our freedom. As we journey through this terrain, we realize that the key to freedom is not to avoid attachment, but to attach mindfully, realizing our own inner completeness, yet embracing life's fluidity. In this wisdom, we find a way to turn our chains into wings.

Opportunity – The Hidden Treasure

"Of all the frictional resistances, the one that most retards human movement is ignorance."
—Nikola Tesla

It's often said that life is a journey full of surprises. This journey is paved with twists and turns, ups and downs, and of course, opportunities. These opportunities may come in the form of a serendipitous meeting, a fortunate event, or even an unexpected challenge. And it is during challenging moments that our capacity to grow and learn may alight.

Life sometimes disguises opportunities as challenges. You may look at a difficult situation and see nothing but despair, when in fact, this could be your biggest opportunity yet. How? Because challenges are the best teachers, catalysts for growth, and above all, they are the wellsprings of transformation. Understanding this concept is the first step to identifying opportunities in challenges.

Thomas Edison once said, "Opportunity is missed by most people because it is dressed in overalls and looks like work." This quote perfectly encapsulates the essence of opportunities hiding in challenges. They aren't always immediately appealing, but beneath the surface lies the potential for meaningful growth and success.

Nikola Tesla, Edison's former protégé, took opportunity to a whole new level when he left a secure position with Edison to snatch his own dream.

Nestled within the heart of Smiljan, a small village in the Croatian hinterland, Tesla was born under a violent thunderstorm in the year 1856. The storm, according to local folklore, was considered a bad omen, foretelling a challenging life. Tesla's mother dismissed this superstition and allegedly said, "He will be a child of light."

Growing up, young Tesla was enchanted by the mysteries of nature. He watched lightning crackle across the darkened sky and felt the vibrations from the ground below, piquing his curiosity about an unseen world. He questioned everything, developing a relentless thirst for knowledge, and spent hours building inventions.

Despite having to confront numerous adversities—an early bout with cholera, the childhood death of his older brother, and limited educational opportunities—Tesla seized every chance he had to learn. He voraciously consumed books, memorizing entire passages. He learned to view his adversities as opportunities to grow stronger. He cured himself of a gambling addiction and refused to quit even when others said his inventions wouldn't work.

Tesla's life took a significant turn when he moved to the United States, drawn by the allure of scientific progress. Despite his initial struggles, he clung to his dream of harnessing the power of nature for mankind—free energy. He seized the opportunity to work with the famed inventor, Thomas Edison, in his burgeoning electric light company.

While this stint was fraught with disagreements and misunderstandings, Tesla emerged undeterred. If something didn't work, he let it go and came up with another way. His ideas were considered radical, even lunatic. He diverged from Edison's direct current (DC) system—and he was often ridiculed—but he continued honing his own concepts anyway. Tesla envisaged an alternate future, powered by alternating current (AC), which he believed would revolutionize the electric industry—and it did.

Tesla's second greatest challenge initially came in the form of a battle: The War of Currents, where his AC system was pitted against Edison's DC. Despite the financial struggles and widespread skepticism, Tesla remained resolute, trusting in his inventions. In a remarkable display of seizing opportunity, he partnered with George Westinghouse, who saw potential in Tesla's ideas. This alliance provided Tesla with the platform he needed to bring his vision to life, culminating in the successful implementation of AC power at the 1893 Chicago World's Fair. The dazzling spectacle of light mesmerized the audience, marking a significant victory for Tesla. And his invention is why we have electricity in our homes today—and the radio—and perhaps—wireless technology, too, if I'm correctly reading his patents.

Tesla's career was dotted with numerous such instances when he met scientific challenges head-on, each time finding opportunities amid scorn, poverty, adversity, and detractors. Tesla never quit.

From the invention of the Tesla coil to his ambitious yet unrealized project, the Wardenclyffe Tower, and his claim to have made connection with extraterrestrials, Tesla's entire life was a testament to creative imagination and relentless spirit. His thoughts also included that women were superior to men because women '*possess unique qualities of mind and soul*'. He predicted that women would ignore precedent and one day startle civilization with their progress. Again, I thank my grandfather for introducing me to this remarkable, forward-thinking visionary.

Nikola Tesla passed away in relative obscurity at the age of eighty-six. Despite the shadows that marred his life, his work ultimately outlived him. Today, Tesla's name resonates with power, success, and innovation. It symbolizes his triumphant journey in transforming challenges into opportunities. He was a rare and true sentient being of light, who seized every thunderstorm that came his way and harnessed them into wireless powerhouses that continue to illuminate our future. His story remains a powerful testament to the adage: In every adversity lies the seed of an equal or greater opportunity.

To identify opportunity, the way Tesla did, we first need to shift our perspective. When faced with a challenge, instead of asking, "Why is this happening to me?" you might consider asking, "What can I learn from this?" or "How can I use this situation to my advantage?" This change in viewpoint will open your eyes to possibilities where others only see obstacles and mire themselves in objection or complaint.

Recognizing an opportunity is only part of the journey; the rest lies in your willingness to embrace opportunity. This is where resilience, creativity, and courage come in. It's easy to shy away from challenges, to choose the path of least resistance and follow a very wide and well-worn path of conformity. Yet, it's by walking through storms, confronting what scares us, that we forge the strongest visions and version of ourselves. It is the hardship and trials we overcome that make the victories more rewarding.

Always remember, the size of an opportunity corresponds with the magnitude of the challenge. Do not be disheartened by the enormity of a problem; instead, be excited about the potential of a solution. Welcome failure and rejection as a data point for learning. For every setback, there is a comeback—if you choose.

. . .

Here are three guiding principles to help you along this journey:

- **Cultivate a Growth Mindset**: A growth mindset refers to the belief that one's abilities and intelligence can be developed through effort, perseverance, and resilience. With this mindset, challenges become less daunting and more inviting, as they present opportunities for self-improvement and learning.

- **Practice Reflection**: Spend time understanding the nature of your challenges. Look for patterns, underlying themes, and lessons to be learned. This introspection allows you to delve deeper into the issue at hand and unearth hidden opportunities.

- **Embrace Uncertainty**: The road less traveled is often the most rewarding. Every great success story involves taking risks and venturing into the unknown.

Strive to embrace the gift of opportunity in every challenge. The difference between those who succeed and those who don't is not the absence of obstacles, but the ability to see past them and into the heart and soul of elevated opportunities.

Reframe and transform your perception of challenges. Instead of seeing everything that's gone wrong and complaining to anyone who really doesn't want to hear you (because they have their own problems, may be cruel, or perhaps do not care), poke through the ashes of your issue and salvage and refurbish potential opportunities. Use change, even if abrupt, or grief, to cut your losses—and step up to your own personal path of success—one you can line with hope and possibility. Your journey is always yours to create, even in the face of conflict, wounds, or overwhelming circumstances. The gift of opportunity awaits you at every turn. Will you raise your energy, frequency, and vibration to seize it?

STRATEGIES FOR MAXIMIZING LIFE'S OPPORTUNITIES

• **Expand your knowledge and skills**: Continuously learn and develop new skills relevant to your interests and goals. This broadens your capabilities and equips you to seize a wider range of opportunities.

• **Cultivate a growth mindset**: Embrace challenges, persevere through setbacks, and view failures as learning opportunities. A growth mindset enables you to approach new experiences with a positive and resilient attitude.

• **Build a strong network**: Connect with diverse individuals in your field of interest or industry. Networking can provide access to valuable opportunities, insights, and collaborations that may not be available otherwise.

• **Embrace curiosity and openness**: Stay curious about the world around you and be open to new ideas, perspectives, and experiences. This mindset allows you to discover opportunities that you might have otherwise overlooked.

• **Set clear goals**: Define your short-term and long-term goals, and regularly review and adjust them as needed. Clear goals help you stay focused and enable you to identify and pursue opportunities that align with your vision.

• **Take calculated risks**: Be willing to step outside your comfort zone and take calculated risks when appropriate. Evaluate potential benefits and drawbacks before making decisions, but don't let fear hold you back from seizing opportunities that could lead to growth and fulfillment.

• **Be proactive and take initiative**: Take the initiative in your personal and professional life by identifying needs, proposing solutions, and being proactive in pursuing your goals.

• **Develop resilience**: Life often presents challenges and setbacks. Building resilience allows you to bounce back from adversity, adapt to changing circumstances, and persevere in the face of obstacles, increasing your chances of finding and capitalizing on opportunities. "No" is more a part of life than "Yes." Rejection is simply a "yes" in waiting.

• **Practice self-reflection**: Regularly take time to reflect on your experiences, values, and aspirations. Reflection helps you stay present and make intentional choices, and identifies opportunities that align with your authentic self.

• **Maintain an optimistic mindset**: Optimism helps you maintain a positive outlook even during challenging times. It enables you to approach situations with a solutions-oriented mindset, increasing your ability to recognize and capitalize on opportunities.

Maximizing life's opportunities is a dynamic process that requires continuous self-improvement, adaptability, and a willingness to explore change.

CONTROL & THE ART OF LETTING GO

"The most difficult thing is the decision to act, the rest is merely tenacity. The fears are paper tigers. You can do anything you decide to do. You can act to change and control your life; and the procedure, the process is its own reward."
—Amelia Earhart

In life, we come across a handful of exceptional individuals who shape and color our existence. Mike H has been one such figure in my life—a beacon of intellect and perception, shining so brightly, he is impossible to overlook.

Our paths didn't cross in a conventional manner; rather, it was Mike who discovered me, pulled in by a research paper I had penned on sex trafficking and the scarcity of reliable governmental data within the strip club industry.

Mike, a private contractor with a rich history in various public agencies, carried the wisdom and precision of an engineer, like my grandfather. An embodiment of resolve and courage, Mike was the kind of man even the most seasoned generals hesitate to challenge. His life is a testament to his tireless commitment to safeguarding humanity, even in the face of Earth's most perilous corners.

Mike's laser-directed anger is also like a bolt of lightning, illuminating harsh truths with such razor-sharp clarity and honesty that you're either spurred to growth or retreat with your ass cheeks burning, so you may improve your argument. He is all about asking the right questions—because life as we know it may depend upon it. He was the mirror that reflected my deepest fears, compelling me to scrutinize them and draw my own conclusions. Mike's interest in me was sparked by a paper I'd written about the strip club industry and sex trafficking, where my aggregated governmental data showed this was not a problem. My data-driven conclusions intrigued him. In a secretive boardroom somewhere in the US, our dialogue flowed under the watchful eyes of an interactive global map.

Before I knew it, Mike had enlisted me in a critical anti-human trafficking initiative under the auspices of the Department of Homeland Security's Science & Technology Directorate. Mine was a fractional piece of a much larger anti-human trafficking foundational effort—but I felt honored to be called upon and treated with respect. Soon, I found myself immersed in the depths of a decommissioned missile silo, ostensibly to understand its history but more so to delve into the depths of Mike's captivating character. Instead, as Mike probably designed, I learned much about myself.

Mike is a believer in simplicity, logic, common sense, and unwavering discipline. He orchestrates his life according to his own rules, yet rarely falls prey to greed or self-centeredness. Demonstrating his compassionate nature, he installed a T-1 line in the Adirondacks during the CV-19 lockdowns to ensure that childhood educations were not compromised.

In ways he may never comprehend, Mike transformed my life. While I had already journeyed far on the path of self-discovery and inner peace, he was instrumental in sharpening my strategic and intelligence skills. But these skills were not to be wielded to destabilize governments. Instead, they serve to rewrite my personal narrative, to relinquish control when needed, to persist, to explore alternatives, and to cherish both surrender and the potency of uncertainty as required—so I may propel beyond them—and improve the lives of others through sound policy. For these are the elements that forge resilience, and in turn, illuminate the paths to strength and overcoming—or winning the greatest of wars—the war with oneself.

In the blink of an eye, Mike had woven me into a network of remarkable women—stellar colonels, pioneering microbiologists, intelligence mavens, combat pilots, and cyber virtuosos. I found myself within a sphere of women who radiated such unshakeable confidence and camaraderie that I knew they'd stand with me on any battlefield. I even received an invitation to a security event at Quantico, where I realized I wanted to learn more from them. These women were the opposite of the compliant, subservient, fearful, and often disgruntled women who marked the landscape of my childhood.

Life, I learned through Mike, is like a game of chess, full of decisions and strategic moves, each one, expected or not, determines the shape of the game —and too, its outcome. But unlike chess, in life, we don't always have full control of the board or the pieces. This illusion of control often leaves us feeling disillusioned, and the first step toward resilience is recognizing this mirage for what it truly is and flipping the board.

The Illusion of Control

Consider a river, a relentless force of nature that shapes its path through mountains and valleys. Deep in the Adirondacks, a river meanders, grows, shrinks, and adapts. Yet, it doesn't control where the rocks fall or how the mountains rise. It only controls its response, shaping its path around the obstacles. We are part of that river. Life is the landscape through which we flow.

In the human experience, control is largely an illusion. While we can manage our actions, reactions, and attitudes, external events remain, for the most part, out of our grasp. We cannot command the weather, dictate the actions of others, or accurately predict global events because these are complex systems. The illusion of control, if left unchecked, leads us down a path of frustration and disappointment.

Embracing the idea that we control less than we think does not mean adopting a pessimistic worldview. Instead, it calls for understanding the dividing line between what is in our hands and what is not, leading us to a more realistic, less stressful, and ultimately more joyful existence.

Embracing Uncertainty

Uncertainty is not an enemy to be defeated, but a reality to be accepted. In uncertainty, we find possibility, growth, and freedom. Where there is uncertainty, there is room for discovery and innovation. And although it can be uncomfortable, that discomfort often signals that we are pushing the boundaries of our comfort zone. Mike expanded my possibilities and fortitude.

Many of our greatest fears derive from uncertainty. We fear the unknown, the unpredictable, the uncertain. When I told Mike I had nothing to offer in skills compared to our comrades, he immediately highlighted my ability for strategic intelligence and said I could share his office address. I never saw those words coming. Again, Mike saw something in me that I'd missed—or perhaps downplayed to keep other workforce playing fields level. In facing and embracing this uncertainty of a new environment, one dedicated to national security and global health, I strengthened my resilience.

When we stop trying to control the uncontrollable and start dancing with the unknown, we realize our capacity for adaptability, creativity, and evolution. Opportunities find us, the way Mike found me, and the way I, metaphorically speaking, found myself.

The Power of Surrender

There is a difference between giving up and surrendering. Giving up implies a loss, a forfeit, a defeat. Surrender, on the other hand, is about release, acceptance, and finding peace amid chaos. Surrendering isn't about passively accepting whatever comes your way; it is about acknowledging what is, and then deciding how to react.

When we surrender, we let go of our insistence on a certain outcome and open ourselves to all possibilities. This doesn't mean we don't aim for goals or strive for success, but rather, we do so with an awareness that the outcome may not always align with our initial desires. And often, this divergence is a source of unexpected blessings.

The power of surrender lies in its ability to free us from the stress and anxiety that come from trying to control the uncontrollable. When we surrender, we find peace in the present moment, we find wisdom in our experiences, we find fortitude in the face of adversity and open ourselves to potentially life-changing opportunity.

The river does not force its path; it flows where it can, adapts when it must, and surrenders to the landscape. Be like the river: Control what you can, embrace uncertainty, and surrender to the journey. Life is not a game to be won or lost but an adventure to be experienced—by most of us—in a cocoon of safety—for others like Mike, winning a game may indeed protect the rest of us so we may safely explore our limits.

Our lives, even Mike's, are works of art in progress, stories that evolve with each passing day. Let go of the illusion of control, embrace the richness of uncertainty, and discover the liberating power of surrender. The beauty of life isn't in the certainty of the destination, but in the mystery and marvel of the quest. Life is not about having all the answers, but about asking the right questions, exploring the possibilities, and growing in fortitude, love, and emotional intelligence along the way.

LONELINESS – THE SILENT ECHO

"Unlike many other illnesses, what I find profoundly empowering about addressing loneliness is that the ultimate solution to loneliness lies in each of us. We can be the medicine that each other needs. We can be the solution other people crave. We are all doctors, and we are all healers."
—Vivek Murthy

Consumed by loneliness, I found myself more isolated than I'd ever been. I was single, pregnant, and impoverished. I watched as my car was repossessed and towed away. I discarded my eviction notice into the trash. The confines of my meager apartment, located above a furniture storage warehouse, mocked me with its sparseness. It was devoid of furniture, save for a diminutive television perched on a plastic nightstand and a threadbare twin mattress without sheets, covered by a second-hand blanket. I didn't even have the luxury of a bed frame.

The lack of material possessions did not wound me as much as the encroaching solitude did, growing dreadful as nightfall approached. The electricity was disconnected, leaving me in a chilling darkness. My kitchen cupboards mirrored my emotional state: barren. Even if I'd had the energy, the nearest store was miles away, a moot point considering I had no money for food. The fading light of day ushered in my tears, which I first fought to keep at bay. I teetered on the brink of homelessness, jobless after losing my bartending gig, and had no familial support. There was no one to call—my phone line was disconnected. I nestled into the cold comfort of the worn blanket and surrendered to my sorrow. The life I led was a byproduct of poor choices, this I knew. But I didn't know what to do about it and lay frozen in helplessness.

My humble dwelling sat on the fringe of a national park forest, just outside of Cleveland, Ohio. Fortunately, it wasn't the icy grip of winter, but a cool, crisp summer night. I stirred from my restless sleep around 3 a.m., lit a candle, and ventured out into the darkness. I trudged a solitary half-mile to a bridge I knew that was nestled amongst an overhang of leafy trees.

A strange thing happens when you hit rock bottom; fear becomes an afterthought. The looming darkness didn't make me afraid. It was the pervasive loneliness that left me petrified. On that bridge, under the soft glow of a single candle, I peered into the river below. A leap would be futile, the current too weak to carry me, the depth inadequate for any kind of planetary escape. With my back against cold stone and steel, I let my tears fall freely. The candle's dim flicker danced against darkness. Left to grapple with my future, I pondered: What would my next move be? It was then I realized, I wasn't alone.

Often, we confuse loneliness with being alone. We perceive them as two faces of the same coin. But there's a chasm of difference between them. Loneliness is an unwelcome state of lack, a feeling of disconnectedness.

Being alone, on the other hand, is merely a physical state of being by oneself. Learning to cherish solitude, to find peace and enrichment in aloneness, can transform your life and lead to a deep sense of well-being.

As we ascend to elevated spirituality and enrichment on our path to self-discovery, we find comfort in solitude. The diversions we previously used to cloak our loneliness lose their allure. Detrimental habits grow dull, and relationships that do not offer support or contribute love to our lives recede, creating space for deeper connections and experiences.

Understanding Loneliness

The roots of loneliness can be traced to our innermost feelings of self-worth, belonging, and love. It does not discriminate based on age, race, or status. From the school kid being bullied to the widow roaming around an empty home, from the seemingly popular Instagram influencer to the successful but isolated CEO—everyone, at some point in their lives, experiences loneliness. Loneliness arises from feeling disconnected or not belonging. Understanding that loneliness is not a life sentence, but a transient state is the first step toward transformation.

The Journey to Solitude

Solitude, unlike loneliness, is not a state of lack but a state of abundance. It's a sanctuary where we nurture our relationship with ourselves. In solitude, we find silence, but not emptiness. We are alone, but it's not loneliness. It's a place where we reconnect with our thoughts, emotions, and spirit, away from the cacophony of the world.

How do we transform loneliness into solitude? It begins with acceptance. Acceptance of our present state of loneliness, not as a flaw or failure, but as an experience from which we can learn and grow—or ask for help.

Next comes self-understanding. We need to delve deep into

ourselves and be honest, to understand our needs, desires, strengths, and vulnerabilities. It is about coming to terms with who we are, warts and all. When we understand ourselves better, we become our own companions, and aloneness ceases to be lonely.

Finally, there's self-love, which is acknowledging your worth and treating yourself with kindness and respect. When we learn to love ourselves, we fulfill our need for love and companionship from within, and solitude becomes a haven, not a prison. I once lamented to a friend that I wished I had loving parents. Without missing a beat, she said, "Be the parent to yourself that you always wanted." I never forgot her words. It led me from loneliness to gratitude for solitude.

Finding Peace in Aloneness

Once we transform loneliness into solitude, we learn to find peace in aloneness. Here are a few ways to cultivate this peace:

• **Self-expression:** Use solitude as a canvas for self-expression. Write, paint, compose music, or indulge in any activity that lets your soul speak. Solitude provides time for purpose and pursuits and offers us a sense of satisfaction that eclipses loneliness.

• **Nature:** Connect with nature. The beauty and tranquility of nature can provide comfort and a sense of belonging, which eases feelings of loneliness.

• **Learning:** Use your alone time to learn and grow. Read a book, learn a new skill, or pursue a hobby. The process of learning keeps the mind engaged and brings a sense of achievement.

Keep in mind, too, that solitude is not about isolating yourself from the world. It's about forming a secure, fulfilling relationship with your inner self. The path from loneliness to solitude is about metamorphizing from inner pain to enlightened splendor, from emptiness to fulfillment. It is about finding peace and contentment within the ability to *inter-see,* and in doing so, transforming your aloneness into a celebration of self-discovery and contentment.

I met an old man on the bridge that night. He was out, he said, for a midnight fish. He carried a tackle box, a fishing pole, and a small cooler. We spoke for a bit, him sensing, I think, my awkwardness and desolation. He handed me an apple and I never tasted one sweeter, savoring every bite right down to the core. I tossed the remnants over the side of the bridge, the splash more of a plink. We stared at the water below in silence.

"You need a ride somewhere?" he finally asked.

"I'm not sure where to go," I said.

"The good Lord always knows the way even if we don't," he said. "And always, angels walk among us."

I never saw him again—but that ride and a stranger's kindness helped save my life.

Freedom – The Ultimate Adventure

"I would like to be remembered as a person who wanted to be free... so other people would be also free."
—Rosa Parks

The chains of oppression manifest in myriad guises. Be it the manacles of slavery, the yoke of tyranny, the blight of corruption, the lash of violence, or the hidden bruises of domestic abuse. Oppression, unfortunately, remains a voracious beast, driven by an insatiable hunger for control and dominion. Freedom, its opposite and majestic phoenix, rises from the ashes of oppression, offering sanctuary from the chilling grasp of abuse and control.

For me, penning an account of freedom proved surprisingly challenging. While my life bore the indelible marks of oppression, it did not know the radioactive rains of a nuclear catastrophe, the deafening thunder of war, or the echoing chains of slavery. In my homeland, the United States, I've always reveled in a level of freedom I have as a woman, freedom woefully denied to many others in distant lands.

In my walk of life, I never had to fear the horrific sentence of a stoning for infidelity, or the constricting imposition of an all-encompassing garment or arranged child marriage. The torch of education never eluded my grasp, nor did a patriarchal decree dictate my personal movements within a country I call home.

Despite bearing the invisible scars of rape and sexual assault, I was spared from the terror of being kidnapped and sex trafficked in a foreign land or being driven from my home to arrive on foreign soil as a reviled or unwelcome refugee. I've never had to seek asylum or been forced into a disease-ridden tent camp or cardboard shelter.

The men and women who helped build my nation's history with their sacrifices, allowed me to voice my grievances about the very framework of this country, without fearing the iron fist of the law or an "accidental" plunge from a high window or balcony. I am conscious of the troubling reality that many of us in the US often overlook these hard-won freedoms. Many of us remain ignorant of the sacrifices our predecessors made so that we could safely and freely voice our discontent or dissent, from the security of our homes or from behind the shield of anonymous (but not) computer screens, with as much inclusiveness and opportunity as the next (pick your pronoun).

Yet, I must acknowledge the sobering truth that not everyone in our nation can bask in the warmth of this freedom. The scale has, for countless generations, tilted in favor of the elites. While the roots of opportunity have taken hold for many of us, they are frequently stunted by forces beyond our grasp—the crippling grip of poverty, the abyss of educational deprivation, inflation, unaffordable housing, copious "fees", the quagmire of politics, corruption, and bureaucracy, the biting winds of raw austerity, and a sometimes-deep-seated prejudice and arrogance anchored in financial stature.

However, amid this apparent bleakness, hope illuminates our path—the freedom of the mind. This realm remains untouched, unowned, no matter how advanced our technology becomes. Only you hold dominion over the thoughts and emotions that reside within the citadel of your heart if you choose to override the unstoppable algorithms of hate, despair, and control coursing through our smart devices. This realm, this sanctuary of consciousness, is yours to nurture, yours to cherish, and our minds, the very embodiment of freedom.

Freedom is a word often tied to physical constructs: the ability to move freely, speak openly, or choose our own path. But true freedom goes beyond the physical realm; it resides in the landscape of our elevated and enlightened inner selves, in our spirit. It's the liberty to think freely, feel deeply, and be genuinely us, unbound by external judgment or internal fear. It's the tranquility that comes from inner peace and harmony—and like water—it does not require use of force.

The Essence of True Freedom

True freedom is the capacity to be authentically and unapologetically us. It's the ability to honor our desires, express our feelings, and assert our beliefs without the fear of rejection, violence, job loss, or judgment. True freedom is about breaking chains in the physical world but also about shattering shackles in the emotional and mental domains: the shackles of fear, injustice, insecurity, guilt, prejudice, regret, and self-doubt.

Freedom includes releasing the weight of mistakes in history and unburdening regrets to liberate ourselves from anxieties about an uncertain future. It's about living in the present, fully, and deeply, with acceptance of what is and what will be.

Pathways to Inner Freedom and Peace

Achieving true freedom is a journey of self-discovery and

transformation. Here are some pathways that can guide you toward inner freedom and peace:

- **Self-awareness:** Self-awareness is the first step toward true freedom. Be conscious of your thoughts, feelings, and actions. Understand your strengths, recognize your weaknesses, and accept your flaws. Self-awareness sheds light on what's holding you back, allowing you to address these barriers on your path to freedom.

- **Forgiveness:** Forgiveness, both toward yourself and others, is a powerful liberator. Release grudges, let go of resentment, and forgive past mistakes. Remember, forgiveness is not about forgetting or condoning; it's about liberating your heart from the chains of bitterness and regret.

- **Authenticity:** Dare to be yourself, despite societal norms or expectations. Embrace your individuality and express it freely. Authenticity is an act of courage that leads to true freedom.

- **Self-love:** Cultivate love and kindness toward yourself. Self-love is not about being self-absorbed or narcissistic; it's about acknowledging your worth, taking care of your needs, and nurturing your well-being. When you love yourself, you set the foundation for inner peace and true freedom.

Remember, true freedom is an *inside* job. It's about changing your circumstances as much as it is about changing your perspective. Freedom is not without rules, responsibility, or constraints but about being at peace despite them.

CHANGE – THE ONLY CONSTANT

"Sometimes if you want to see a change for the better, you have to take things into your own hands."
—Clint Eastwood

Many years ago, I held a position on the board of the PACE Center for Girls, situated in the agricultural heart of Immokalee, Florida. The center stood proud among a surrounding of ramshackle buildings, its foundations firmly rooted in nine inviolable principles, ranging from honoring the female spirit to cherishing integrity and relentlessly pursuing excellence. These were the compass points of our mission. PACE is an alternative school for *at-risk* girls between the ages of 12-17.

One memorable initiative was christened "Breakfast & Books." It was during this time that I found myself assigned to mentor Dee, a spirited twelve-year-old storm brewing a steady tempest of anger. To be a girl growing up in Immokalee was a challenge, and Dee had already faced trials that would terrify the most seasoned of adults. Her entrance into the room was permeated with a tangible reluctance, a certain skepticism. What could a young African American girl possibly learn from an older white woman, one who appeared utterly detached from the realities of Dee's existence? I shared some of my past with her to break the ice. Dee was surprised I'd been a foster child and ward of the court. We rarely discussed the books we'd read, except for maybe how we might use their lessons to each better our lives. One thing I knew, Dee was smart—smart enough to go to college. She was resilient and she was a fighter. It was only the labels assigned to her and the dire circumstances of her life that held her in place. How could we, together, get those tough variables to budge and move them out of her way?

Despite the murky waters of Dee's private struggles, our conversations ran clear and true. We acknowledged the harsh reality that life would not roll out a red carpet for her—she would have to fight, to push through the rubble of her circumstances and toil harder than anyone else she knew. I impressed upon her the power of education, the shiny key that could unlock a world beyond the constricting boundaries of Immokalee. For this, she would need to befriend change, altering her perceptions, her surroundings, and her ambitions.

Trust wasn't something that came naturally to Dee. A trail of shattered promises and disappointments lay behind her. However, as time painted our story, I was privileged to witness her metamorphosis from a seriously troubled child to a proud high school graduate, her name inked on the honor rolls of both success and great spirit. Unseen by her, my eyes welled up with pride at her graduation ceremony.

Fast forward to her post-high school days, and she had a college scholarship within her grasp. But she was hampered by a lack of transportation from Immokalee to Fort Myers and *wait-listed* for a dorm room.

"I'm going to have to give up college for a while. If I don't go this fall, I lose my scholarships."

"To hell you will!" I yelled into the phone. I was adamantly against her giving up and made a fervent pledge to find a solution. I'd told her for years that education was her ticket to a better life. I couldn't be the next person to plant another false promise in the field of her hope. My pleas for help were met with a disheartening response. People offered to give her rides to a local casino or to the fields if she wanted to work—but there were no buses or rides to Ft. Myers from Immokalee. Dee's dream seemed to teeter on the edge of collapse. I felt a sense of guilt creeping in as I feared I might join the ranks of those who had let her down.

A beacon of hope appeared in the form of Steve K., a contact I knew from Leadership Collier. He introduced me to Naples Auto Donation, a charitable organization that offered vehicles to those in need. However, they were not free. Through the power of the collective, we crowdfunded for Dee's car and insurance, ensuring her journey to academic triumph could continue, if she maintained a B average at school.

Dee drove her 2001 Buick right up to the hallowed halls of her college graduation. Today, she stands tall, a master's degree in public health in her hands. Against insurmountable odds, Dee didn't just defy her circumstances; she rewrote the celestial map, shifting her stars and creating her own universe of possibilities.

Whenever I confront the winds of change, I remember Dee, her indomitable spirit, and her inspiring journey. And in the face of any adversity, I am inspired anew.

Change, often regarded with trepidation, is a part of life. Developing strategies to adapt to change, as Dee did, not only equips you to navigate life's twists and turns with grace but also opens doors to evolution and opportunities.

The Inevitability of Change

Change is as inevitable as the rising sun. Life is a dynamic, ever-evolving process. Seasons change, civilizations rise and fall, and even the universe is in a constant state of flux. Likewise, we change—our bodies, our minds, our circumstances, our relationships. Change can be gradual, like the aging process, or abrupt, like the end of a relationship or the start of a new job.

Fear of change is natural and common. We fear the unknown, we fear losing control, we fear that change will bring pain or discomfort. However, viewing change as a menacing force limits our growth and robs us of the chance to learn, evolve, and experience new things.

Understanding the inevitability of change helps us appreciate it as a natural and necessary part of life. Change challenges us. It closes old doors, but it opens new ones. It ends certain chapters in our lives, but it also begins new ones.

Embracing Change: Strategies for Adaptability

Embracing change doesn't mean ignoring the discomfort or pain it may bring. Rather, it's about acknowledging these feelings and using strategies to adapt and thrive. Here are some strategies to cultivate adaptability:

- **Acceptance:** Accepting change is a part of life helps you embrace it. Acceptance doesn't mean passive resignation; it's a conscious acknowledgment of reality, a necessary step before any positive action occurs.

- **Perspective Shift:** Reframe how you view change. See it as an opportunity for growth and learning, the way Dee did. Each change carries a lesson, and each transition is an invitation to evolve.

- **Flexibility:** Cultivate a flexible mindset. Flexibility allows you to adjust your sails according to the wind, helping you to effectively navigate obstacles, setbacks, and unexpected events.

- **Preparedness:** While we can't predict every change that occurs, we can build emotional and practical preparedness. Maintain a strong support system, develop resilience, and manage your resources wisely.

- **Self-Care:** During times of change, self-care becomes even more crucial. Ensure you're eating well, exercising regularly, getting enough sleep, and making time for relaxation and activities you enjoy.

- **Seeking Support:** Don't hesitate to seek support. Share your feelings with a trusted friend or family member, join a support group, or consider speaking with a mental health professional. It's okay to seek help or lean on others when navigating change.

Embracing change is not always easy. It requires courage, resilience, and patience—the latter something Dee has much more of than I do! Yet, in doing so, we find opportunities to discover new aspects of ourselves and the world. As we cultivate adaptability, we not only survive change but thrive in it, emerging stronger, wiser, and more resilient.

Death—A Leap into the Unknown

"When your time comes to die, be not like those whose hearts are filled with fear of death, so that when their time comes, they weep and pray for a little more time to live their lives over again in a different way. Sing your death song and die like a hero going home."
—Tecumseh

For many years, I have worked as a consultant for the strip club industry. My choice to represent the freedoms of such an industry, especially when I've also consulted on matters of national security, often draws confusion and skepticism from outsiders who question my involvement in a sector they deem dubious. I, however, am a fervent believer in freedom. Just as we champion liberty overseas, we should respect our freedoms at home, which include the autonomy of individuals who choose this line of work.

In an ironic twist, it's not uncommon for legislation introduced under the guise of protecting strippers to further stigmatize them instead. For instance, there are laws in the US that prohibit women from approaching men within six feet in a strip club, that impose midnight closures, restrict alcohol, or prohibit tipping. Sometimes, the laws result in hefty fines, or 1st degree misdemeanors for women (but not the men), equivalent in some states to vehicular homicide. These are not empowering measures, but rather, constraints that hinder the agency of women viewed as "less than."

Additionally, I've never been a fan of forcing women to become victims of minimum wage. Perhaps women wouldn't resort to stripping if our elected officials spent more time crafting genuine job growth or educational policies over banning behavior that some of their most zealot constituents will always deem reprehensible. These types of laws, to me, represent spiritual snobbery and legislating morality rather than serving a bona fide governmental purpose, as laws are supposed to do.

My understanding of freedom and sacrifice took on a deeper meaning after an encounter with Sgt. Linda Pierre, a member of the 101st Special Troops Battalion, 101st Sustainment Brigade, 101st Airborne Division, Fort Campbell, Ky. Our paths crossed during a turbulent flight from Florida to Atlanta.

In her uniform, Sgt. Pierre was the picture of strength and courage. During the worst turbulence, she held my hand, laughing that if I thought this was bad, I should try flying out of Afghanistan, where vertical climbs to dodge missile fire were the norm. We spoke at length about her life, her Haitian heritage, her military service, and her enduring love for her family and the opportunities the Army provided her.

When we landed, I gave her my business card and told her to reach out if she ever needed anything. I never anticipated the grand impact this gesture would have on my life and the lives of countless others.

A few months later, Sgt. Pierre found herself deployed to Afghanistan. With Christmas approaching and morale waning among her unit, she reached out to me for assistance. Despite my initial apprehensions, I resolved to honor her request.

I turned to the very industry others often disparage and deride. The strip club owners and operators, without hesitation, contributed generously to our cause. Together, we managed to airlift over 300 boxes of supplies to Sgt. Pierre's unit just in time for Christmas. Her email conveyed the gratitude of her unit, and it filled me with pride to see the exemplary generosity of the strip club industry and the impact it had on the lives of our brave servicemen and servicewomen. We set a place for her at our Christmas dinner table that year. I told her it would be here for her when she returned.

After the New Year in 2011, Sgt. Pierre emailed me to say she was being deployed to an undisclosed location and would "go dark" for a while. She admitted she was frightened but was the first to volunteer for this dangerous assignment.

A few weeks later, a ding on my cell phone. It was a news push from the BBC that stated five NATO troops had been killed in Afghanistan. I bolted upright, looked at my husband, and said, "Linda's dead." He looked at my phone. He then told me that no names were mentioned in the article, that lots of troops were fighting in Afghanistan, and it probably wasn't her.

I can't tell you how I knew, a feeling I guess, but I ran to the computer and fired off an email to Linda, asking if she was all right. She'd previously said she wouldn't have access to email, but I prayed for a response. None arrived.

Later that evening, my father-in-law, a former federal agent who'd once served as the attaché to the Roman embassy, confirmed to my husband that Sgt. Linda Pierre had indeed lost her life to a Taliban member posing as an Afghan soldier. I sank to the floor of our bedroom, pulling the bedsheets with me, the anguish unbearable—and if it was hard for me, I could not imagine how this terrible news impacted her parents.

Sgt. Pierre's demise was at the hands of a Taliban insurgent. Her bravery and sacrifice moved me to tears, and I found myself sharing the tragic news with the strip club industry that had so recently rallied behind her. The genuine outpouring of love, respect, and support from adult club professionals was immense.

Her funeral was a poignant moment for me. As I eulogized Sgt. Pierre, her mother paused her grieving to look at me. After the service, I had the honor of meeting Linda's family, comrades, and superiors, whom we escorted to the cemetery. Sgt. Pierre was posthumously awarded a Bronze Star and a Purple Heart for her heroic act of jumping on a grenade to protect her subordinates.

During our flight together, Linda confessed her fear of dying, but also affirmed her readiness to sacrifice herself for her brothers and sisters in arms. It was an admission that stirred intense respect and admiration within me, and it solidified the lesson Linda left me with, which is the importance of valuing this blip of a gift called life and making the most of it while you can.

Though Sgt. Linda Pierre's life tragically ended in Afghanistan on April 16, 2011, her spirit lives on in the lives she touched. Her courage, sacrifice, and the lessons she taught me have greatly shaped my outlook. In honoring her memory, I continue to champion freedom and respect in every facet of my life and work.

Death, despite being an inevitable part of our human journey, is often shrouded in fear and uncertainty. But what if we reframe our understanding of death, the way Linda did—not as a terrifying end but as a transition, a passage into the unknown, that post-grief, may offer some comfort?

Death: Neither Beginning nor End, but Transition

There's a truth in the saying, "The only certainties in life are death and taxes." But death, the Buddhists tell me, is not an end but a transition—much like birth. Just as birth marks the transition from the womb to the world, death marks the passage from the physical world to a realm we have yet to comprehend fully.

Our fear of death typically stems from our fear of the unknown. We fear what we cannot see, touch, control, or understand. We fear the cessation of our consciousness, and the finality of our existence. Yet, change and transition are natural parts of life and millions of sentient beings have gone before us. The seasons change, the day turns into night, caterpillars transform into butterflies—change and transition are everywhere, and they are beautiful.

If we accept that death, like birth, is just another transition, we begin to see it not as a dreadful end but as a leap into the unknown. It's the completion of one journey and the beginning of another, much like closing a book after the final page and picking up a new one.

In Mexico, the colorful celebration of Día de los Muertos, or Day of the Dead, is perhaps one of the most recognized commemorations of deceased loved ones worldwide. The holiday mixes a cornucopia of indigenous Aztec beliefs and Catholicism brought by Spanish colonizers. It is a vibrant, multi-day celebration taking place from October 31 to November 2. Families craft altars loaded with marigolds, candles, and photographs of the dead, and adorn each altar with the departed's favorite meals and drinks. Pan de Muerto, considered bread of the dead, and other sweets are shared in the spirit of celebration. The belief is that the spirits return to partake in these earthly delights, reaching across the spiritual divide.

In contrast, the Japanese observe Obon, a Buddhist event during summer, to honor their ancestors. The celebration includes household and temple altars and offerings and cleaning the graves of ancestors. As part of the ceremony, floating lanterns, known as Tōrō Nagashi, are released into rivers, symbolizing the return of spirits to the underworld. The entire event is characterized by a mix of solemn respect and joyous reunion, captured by the Bon Odori—a dance that invites the spirits to enjoy and celebrate life.

Madagascar's Famadihana, or the "turning of the bones," is likely the most unique way I've ever seen of honoring the dead. Every five to seven years, families gather to exhume the wrapped remains of their ancestors, clean them, replace their burial clothes, and dance with the bodies to live music before reburial. This direct and tactile interaction with the dead is a reminder of the unity that binds the past and the present, and reinforces the notion of death as a continuing part of the circle of life.

In Ghana, the Ga-Adangbe people create elaborate coffins called "abebuu adekai," which means "boxes with proverbs." Coffins are shaped and decorated to reflect the life, work, or personality of the deceased. For example, if one was a builder, they might be buried in a coffin shaped like a house. This practice represents a celebration of the person's life and serves as a representation of their identity in the afterlife.

When we take the time to honor and remember our ancestors, we honor ourselves and add light to our lives. Reverence, veneration, and death commemoration are testimonies to humanity's quest for understanding and coming to terms with the ephemeral nature of life. But they are also moments of strength for the living. When I think about Linda Pierre, and her death, I connect with her memory, and it inspires me to live well.

Consequently, when I learned about my 10th great-grandfather Iliam Dhone Christian, a former governor of the Isle of Man who was unjustly executed on Hango Hill in June 1663 for defending tribal lands from royal takeover, I drew grit and determination from my roots. Our heritage is important—and so is our true history.

It has often been said that history, unfortunately, repeats itself. I have higher hopes for this planet. As of today, it is the only one we have capable of sustaining our lives. I know of no other place off planet that can sustain human life and its companionate plants, animals and insects.

Each culture, in its unique way, maintains bonds with those who have passed on, keeping their memories alive in their hearts, minds, and stories. These practices serve to remind us that even in death, we are a part of a continuum, inextricably connected to those who have come before us, and those who will follow.

Finding Comfort Within the Inevitable

Understanding death as a transition may provide some comfort, but how can we cultivate this understanding and find peace with death's inevitability when tragedy strikes? Here, I wish I had magic words. None exist. If we lose a child or a close loved one, I can only offer that it is a soul pain so concentrated and deep, we must heavily grieve. The sudden death of a loved one or family member is an automatic and primal response for the ones left behind and is akin to having a piece of your heart torn away. Mere words cannot cure the abrupt departure death sometimes brings. To me, such gut-wrenching heartbreak is another unbridled manifestation of the deepest of loves and must be expressed.

Here are some ways to potentially cope with death:

- **Reflect on Life:** Reflection on the transient nature of life can bring about a sense of peace regarding death. Contemplating the beauty, complexity, and impermanence of life can help us accept death as a natural part of existence.

- **Express Your Feelings:** Discuss your thoughts and fears about death with a trusted friend, family member, or mental health professional. It can be therapeutic to share your feelings and fears about death, and such conversations can also provide new perspectives.

• **Get in Touch with your Spirit:** Engaging in spiritual practices or philosophies can provide a greater understanding and acceptance of death. Practices like meditation, prayer, chanting, mantras, or reading spiritual texts can foster peace and acceptance.

• **Live Fully:** To mitigate the fear of death, live fully in the present. Recognize the beauty around you, appreciate the moments you have, and create a life filled with purpose and joy. As Eleanor Roosevelt once said, "The purpose of life is to live it, to taste experience to the utmost, to reach out eagerly and without fear for newer and richer experience."

• **Plan for Your Own Transition:** Think about your wishes regarding end-of-life care or funeral arrangements. Having a plan provides a sense of control and peace of mind, for you and for the others you'll leave behind.

• **Cultivate Gratitude:** Embrace gratitude for the life you have. Gratitude has a transformative power that can help you appreciate the journey of life, thereby easing fears associated with its end.

Death, much like life, is a safari. It's an unexplored passage into the unknown. Accepting death as a natural part of life may alleviate our fears and bring comfort when we meet the inevitable. And it's during that time we seek comfort that we truly live.

The Harmony of Elevated Living & Holistic Integration

"He who lives in harmony with himself lives in harmony with the universe."
—Marcus Aurelius

As we enter the final vortex of this cosmic safari, we reflect on every chapter we've traversed, every insight gleaned, and every chord struck in the symphony of our existence. The enigma of existence, the sands of time, love, emptiness, dreams, spirit, faith, consciousness, fear, integrity, credibility, value, attachment, opportunity, control, loneliness, freedom, change, and death—all of these are not isolated elements or emotions of limited lives, but interconnected photons that brighten our souls, hearts, and eyes with light. I tell no stories here—but invite you to craft your own.

Living in harmony with your inner heart and your outer environment is the ultimate key to holistic integration and human elevation. It is the music we create when all facets of our existence—physical, emotional, spiritual—resonate together, in a choir that is mirrored by the frequencies and vibrations of the universe.

When we allow ourselves to loosen our lotus and open our hearts to the melodies of self-discovery and peace, we begin to *inner-see* that our lives are much more than the sum of their phases. We are a complex composition of existence, playing our symphony of frequencies and vibrations among an infinite cosmos, as composer and composition, and part of a much bigger concert.

The light within each of us resonates its rays reach out to the corners of the universe, reflecting our essence back to us in an infinite number of brilliant ways. As sentient beings, we dance with planet Earth among the cosmos, along an infinite quantum electrical feedback loop, a spiral of creation that involves exalted harmony between order and chaos. This is the reality of holistic integration—the acknowledgment that we are interdependent beings in an interconnected universe, where every thought, word, and action, like the wings of a monarch butterfly, really does produce a ripple effect and makes an impact.

Within our human construct of time, we realize that each moment of our lives is precious, and our personalities a distinct note that will never be played in the same way again within this universe. As we foster love within ourselves and toward others, we become conduits of Source, igniting this world with our fire, love, and compassion. Emptiness becomes a canvas for creation, a stage where our dreams and dramas freely unfold through time and space, fueled by the flame of our inner spirit.

Our understanding of God and faith becomes a personal symphony, too, not bound by doctrine but by a direct, intimate experience with the sacred. Through the gateways of consciousness, we witness the grand spectacles, illusions, and alternate realities of life, with all its highs, lows, joys, sorrows, and parallel dimensions. We begin to see fear not as an enemy, but as a teacher guiding us toward courage.

Integrity becomes our melody, credibility our harmony, and self-value our rhythm, giving us the confidence to perform our life's dance with authenticity and pride. As we understand the nature of attachment, we strike the right chords in our relationships, creating a beautiful composition of love and respect.

We open the hidden doors of opportunity, ready to embrace uncertainty and let go of our illusions of control. We transmute loneliness into solitude, understanding that being alone doesn't have to mean feeling lonely. We embark on the quest for inner freedom, embracing change as our ally, and finally, recognizing death as a part of the melody, a part of life's transition into the unknown abyss—where our energy is never destroyed but transformed.

And as this cosmic symphony plays on, we come to realize that we are not just spectators, but active participants in this magnificent ensemble called life. We are more than blips of notes on sheet music. We are the music, too—even as we transition off this planet into some new form of energy, frequency, and vibration.

As you unfasten your personal restraints, remember that every ending is a new beginning. The question is, how will you choose to proceed under the soft glow of enlightenment? Will you embrace the melody of life, dance to its rhythm, and let your spirit resonate with its harmony—or lie down and let life plop its claws over your head? Remember, *inter-seeing* and 'just being' is never about reaching a destination, but about enjoying the quest, about losing yourself in the music, and switching on your inner light under a melody of stars. Craft your story. Will it be an adventure? A drama? A tragedy? Or a fairy tale?

Like the lotus, it is my hope you'll continue to rise out of the mud, toward the sun, open your heart to self-discovery and peace, and let your soul music play. As a unique melody, you are essential and profoundly beautiful—and you are loved. Go ahead. Take the quantum leap and loosen your lotus!

Acknowledgments

First and foremost, I want to extend my heartfelt gratitude to my editor, Michael Waitz, whose dedication, and sharp insights shaped this book into its final form. His patience and expertise were invaluable in this journey. Michael is a New Orleans native. He holds a BA in English from the University of New Orleans and an MA in Homeland Security from the American Military University. Mike served ten years in US Air Force Reserve Public Affairs; wore an editor's hat for twelve years at a large legal publisher; and has enjoyed almost a decade as editor and owner of Sticks and Stones Freelance Editing. He and his family live near Boone, North Carolina.

I extend my deepest gratitude to Colonel Jennifer Aupke, the Division Chief for Irregular Warfare and Special Operations at the Air National Guard in Washington, DC, and the Co-Founder of The Milieux Project, Inc. Her dedication, passion, and relentless commitment to connecting girls and women to aviation opportunities have been instrumental to this project. (Jennifer, I have no doubt that your 'next phase of life' will take you to record-breaking and breathless heights.)

Colonel Aupke's impressive career, marked by her service as an instructor helicopter pilot with over 1800 hours of flying time, six deployments, 76 credited saves, and the courageous earning of the Air Force Combat Action Medal, stands as a testament to her exceptional leadership and valor. A 2001 graduate of the United States Air Force Academy, her 18 years of active duty and multiple leadership roles within the National

Guard reveal a remarkable journey filled with achievements and contributions.

I sincerely thank Colonel Jennifer Aupke for her invaluable support, insights, and inspiration in writing the foreword for this book. Her wisdom and experience have enriched these pages, and her ongoing work continues to pave the way for future generations. For more information about Colonel Aupke's incredible charity, please visit The Milieux Project.

I would like to extend my heartfelt gratitude to Ashley Ruggirello of Cardboard Monet for her incredible work on the cover design of this book. Her artistic vision, passion, and relentless attention to detail have resulted in a cover that's not just visually stunning but also encapsulates the essence of the stories within.

I also want to thank 2Portal Publishing for their belief in this project and unwavering support. As a boutique publishing group based in Naples, Florida, 2Portal Publishing is known for its specialization in science fiction, fantasy fiction, and inspirational non-fiction. With a commitment to fostering original voices and innovative ideas, 2Portal Publishing serves as a hub for readers who seek the thrill, the life-altering, and the thought-provoking.

I would like to extend my sincerest thanks to Dr. Lori Settle for her offer of technical support and collaboration on my sci-fi novels. Her remarkable intelligence and extensive background as a microbiologist, and in the field of national security, are nothing short of transformative in shaping my works that revolve around intelligent female leaders. Her insights and guidance both inform and enrich my content in ways that words alone cannot adequately convey. Dr. Settle, your offer and your expertise is deeply appreciated, and this work stands as a testament to your generous time and contributions.

I would like to extend heartfelt gratitude to Mike Hopmeier of Unconventional Concepts Inc. Mike's support was more than professional; it was a personal testament to the belief that we all have hidden potentials, waiting to be unlocked. His confidence in my abilities, and particularly in my knack for strategic intelligence, was not just an ego boost but a lantern in moments of doubt. He saw in me a destiny for greater things, and his belief is often the wind beneath my wings. He has served as a technical advisor and operational consultant to numerous governmental agencies including the DARPA Defense Sciences Office, U.S. Army Medical Research and Materiel Command, United States Surgeon General, and the Deputy Assistant to the Secretary of Defense for Chemical and Biological Defense. He was one of the primary developers of the Bioterrorism Preparedness Program at the CDC, served as the Science and Technology Advisor to the USAF Surgeon General, as well as the first S&T Advisor to the United States Marine Corps Chem/Bio Incident Response Force (CBIRF). He has been a member and/or task force Chair for numerous senior advisory panels including the Defense Science Board and the National Academy of Sciences and served on the Senior Policy and Strategy Panel for Lawrence Livermore National Laboratory.

A renowned epidemiologist and former undersecretary of health, Dr. Timothy Davis, M.D. graciously made himself available too, sharing his vast knowledge and experience without reservation. His research and insights add layers of scientific depth and authenticity to my work. Additionally, his dedication to our health and well-being is as remarkable as his professional accolades. He is our guardian and guide, keeping us focused, safe, and inspired, while we traverse complex subject matter.

In the unique fabric of support and compassion that binds us together as a community, there are sometimes threads that go unnoticed or omitted. It is my great honor to bring attention to some of those threads, woven together in a story of empathy, compassion, and unselfish giving, which unfolded during Christmas 2010.

I wish to express my deepest and sincerest gratitude to the strip club owners, executives, and dancers across the United

States, who demonstrated an unparalleled spirit of benevolence and solidarity in supporting Sgt. Linda Pierre's unit in Afghanistan.

During a time when those serving abroad long for warmth and family, the strip club community extended their hands across the sea, delivering not only care packages but also emotional support and a sense of belonging to those brave souls far from home. Your generosity and thoughtfulness lit up some dark and desolate nights in the desert, filling soldiers with hope for humanity and greater camaraderie.

The adult club industry is often misunderstood. It is my hope your generosity (if you work in this industry), sheds light on your overlooked charitable efforts, such as purchasing a safe house for domestic violence victims in Charlotte NC and allowing charities into your establishments to offer services and ministering to dancers—and also for offering seniors and veterans free lunches in clubs or providing food for hungry families in need and conducting toy drives for the Marine Corp. or donating to cancer victims.

The kindness exhibited by the strip club community reaches beyond the confines of Afghanistan, touching many lives across our nation. The philanthropy of the strip club industry provides for the marginalized, feeds the hungry, and supports causes that go largely unnoticed. It's time your deeds were recognized.

Let us also take a moment to appreciate the artistry, strength, and resilience of the dancers, who extend themselves beyond the stage, contributing their time, resources, and energy to causes that truly matter. Your grace transcends the physical realm, reaching into the very soul of humanity.

To Sgt. Linda Pierre and her unit, who connected with these unexpected allies. Your open-hearted acceptance of this unconventional support is a testament to the unity and unbreakable bonds that make us strong as a nation. I miss you, Linda. I strive to honor your memory and sacrifice each day by making the most of this life I've been gifted. You've shown me bravery in the face of death and unbound love in the heart of a true warrior.

I am deeply grateful to Thích Nhất Hạnh, the Vietnamese Zen master and peace activist. Thích Nhất Hạnh is known for his teachings on Buddhism, love, and peace. He played a significant role in introducing mindfulness practices to the Western world and applying the principles of his faith to worldly problems. He authored numerous books on anger, fear, communication, and living your best life. His works continue to inspire me. Thich transitioned from this planet on January 22, 2022, at the age of ninety-five. I am the *Angelina* to Thay's *David.* And I have overcome my anger (most of the time).

The encouragement from my friends and family was a constant source of strength too. To my best friend and husband David, who stood by me during late nights and early mornings, and our six children, who are always understanding, thank you from the bottom of my heart. I also want to acknowledge my dear friends, Carla Mills and Mindy DiPietro, who offered continual encouragement and a listening ear.

I must also express my gratitude to men and women in selfless service to our nation, whose sacrifices and dedication help keep us safe, free, and able to protest, dissent, worship (or not), and to live, dress, love and complain or cancel if we please. Your commitment to fostering peace and maintaining the front lines of freedom is truly appreciated—and this goes for the special federal agents and victim assistance specialists at Homeland Security Investigations too, for your relentless pursuit of excellence in the field, and your constant reinforcement and promotion of a victim-centered approach to rescuing victims of human trafficking.

I want to extend a special acknowledgment to those who shared their personal stories and experiences, adding depth and humanity to this work. Your voices are the soul of this book, especially you Max, for your quiet generosity and abundant capacity for non-judgmental love.

I wish to thank you, the reader, for your interest and engagement with this work. It is for you that this book exists, and I hope it serves you well.

Lastly, I thank my "Uncle" Franklin—you know why, and you're stuck with me!

With sincere thanks,

B.A. Crisp

About the Author

B.A. Crisp is more than an accomplished author and CEO; she's a living embodiment of resilience, perseverance, and the pursuit of justice. Leading the Washington, D.C.-based consulting company, Crisp Concepts, Inc., she has forged a path marked by innovation, empathy, and an unyielding commitment to make a difference.

A survivor-turned-'thriver', Crisp's experiences have shaped her into a powerful advocate against the grave injustice of human trafficking. As a private sector advisor to the Dept. of Homeland Security's Science & Technology Directorate, she lent her expertise to a federal anti-human trafficking foundational effort and has worked with federal law enforcement. Her dedication was recognized with a nomination for the 2015 Homeland Security Director's Service Award, for her relentless pursuit of the mandates set by the White House and Congress in the battle against human trafficking.

Crisp's literary portfolio is as profound as her advocacy work. Her Amazon #1 bestseller, "Red Bird," stands as a testament to her storytelling prowess, followed by the captivating novel "X Point," and her much-anticipated third book, "Emergent," released in March 2023.

In her versatile career, Crisp has acted as an advisor for private contractors in national security and served as a Psychiatric Assessment Specialist, helping implement and test mental health-based diagnostic software. As a former vetted volunteer with the Collier County Sheriff's Office, she's been on the frontline of the battle against human trafficking and crisis intervention, translating her personal experiences into tangible action and measurable solutions.

Educationally, Crisp's brilliance shines through her Associate of Arts Degree from Cuyahoga Community College, a B.A. in psychology from Ursuline College, where she graduated Summa cum Laude, and an M.S. from George Washington University's Graduate School of Political Management as co-valedictorian. Her studies extended to the prestigious Exeter College, University of Oxford, U.K., and the London School of Journalism, adding to her multifaceted skillset.

As a former ward of the court and foster child, Crisp's journey from adversity to triumph is inspiring. Her life is a testament of sincere and genuine resonance, which courses through her work, her advocacy, and her life. Her legacy isn't about the accolades or titles she's earned, but in the lives she continues to impact, the minds she has opened, and the positive change she continues to inspire. B.A. Crisp's story reminds us that no matter the obstacles we face, with courage, determination, and the drive to thrive, we can reshape our destiny.

To learn more about B.A. Crisp and her books, please visit: www.bacrisp.com

Resources

Resources:
National Human Trafficking Hotline
Hours: 24 hours, 7 days a week. Languages: English, Spanish.
888-373-7888

988 Suicide and Crisis Hotline
If you or someone you know is struggling or in crisis, call or text 988 or chat 988lifeline.org
For veterans: Available 24/7: Dial 988 then Press 1, chat live, or
text 838255

National Domestic Violence Hotline
Hours: 24/7. Languages: English, Spanish and 200+
1-800-799-7233

National Sexual Assault Hotline: Confidential 24/7 Support: 1-800-656-HOPE

Reloshare: https://www.reloshare.com/ For agencies and NGO's looking for anonymous victim safe shelter placement

Made in United States
Orlando, FL
11 October 2023

37787828R00109